Social Economics

SOCIAL ECONOMICS

Market Behavior in a Social Environment

GARY S. BECKER

KEVIN M. MURPHY

THE BELKNAP PRESS OF HARVARD UNIVERSITY PRESS

CAMBRIDGE, MASSACHUSETTS, AND LONDON, ENGLAND   2000

Library of Congress Cataloging-in-Publication Data

Becker, Gary Stanley, 1930–
    Social economics : market behavior in a social environment / Gary S. Becker,
Kevin M. Murphy.
        p.   cm.
    Includes bibliographical references and index.
    ISBN 0-674-00337-3 (alk. paper)
    1. Economics—Sociological aspects.   2. Social interaction—Economic aspects.
I. Murphy, Kevin M.   II. Title.

HM548 .B43 2000
306.3—dc21   00-057895

*To our late friend Jim Coleman,
who pioneered the integration of
social forces and rational choice*

Contents

Acknowledgments

We have received generous financial support for our research during the past several years on the interaction between market behavior and social forces. We especially want to acknowledge the support of the National Institute for Child Health and Development (grant number HD22054-11), the Olin Foundation grant to the University of Chicago to study the formation of preferences and values, and the George Stigler Center for the Study of the Economy and the State. Becker received generous support for his research from the Hoover Institution.

Three chapters were written in full collaboration with others. William Landes is coauthor of Chapter 6, which analyzes how social forces can enormously raise the prices of certain paintings, antiques, and various "collectibles." Edward Glaeser coauthored Chapter 7, on how competition to consume the same goods as leaders may greatly escalate the quality of goods that leaders consume. Iván Werning is coauthor of Chapter 8 on the links between status, gambling, and the inequality of incomes.

We benefited from the presentation of different chapters at various seminars and conferences, and received valuable comments from Francisco Buera, Guity Nashat, Richard Posner, Sherwin Rosen, and Robert Topel. Students and colleagues, and the general research atmosphere provided by the University of Chicago Department of Economics and Graduate School of Business, could not have been better.

Victor Lima, Rodrigo Suares, and Iván Werning provided excellent research assistance and useful suggestions. Iván gave valuable general comments on, and corrected several errors in, Chapter 5. Elizabeth Gilbert was an outstanding editor, Sandra Wesolowski contributed essential secretarial services, and Michael Aronson helped with the title and many other challenging problems of transforming our work into a book.

We believe that this study makes significant progress in understanding social markets, yet we are also painfully aware that many unsolved issues remain. Instead of waiting to solve some of them, we decided to publish now in the hope of stimulating additional research by others.

PART I

The Effect of Social Capital on Market Behavior

The Importance of Social Interactions

1. Introduction

Modern economics, whether in textbooks or in the most advanced journal articles, typically assumes that individual behavior is not *directly* influenced by the actions of others. Of course, it is understood that every individual is greatly affected *indirectly,* since the behavior of other persons and of firms determines the relative prices of different goods, the rewards to different kinds of labor and capital, marital prospects, political programs, and most other aspects of economic, social, and political life.

While these indirect effects are enormously important, they do not capture fully the influence of others on a person's behavior. Presumably for this reason, anthropologists and sociologists have repeatedly told economists about the importance of culture, norms, and social structure. Economists have not listened, however, mainly because these other fields have not developed powerful techniques for analyzing social influences on behavior.

Yet endless examples attest to the great impact of culture, norms, and social structure. Popular restaurants and books are determined in good part by what is considered "in"; a teenager's propensity to take drugs and to smoke is very much affected by whether his peers do; a person's preference for political candidates is affected by polls stating who is more popular; whether an unmarried mother applies for welfare is influenced by whether many women in her neighborhood are collecting welfare; the popularity of particular types of clothing, designer watches, painting and architectural styles, and even ideas is dependent on the tastes of fashion and intellectual "leaders"; how well children treat their elderly parents is determined by what other children are doing, and by the traditional way of treating parents of past generations; whether a person is honest is very much affected by the teachings of parents and religion, and by traditions inherited from the past.

The activities, behavior, and consumption most subject to strong social pressures from peers and others are those that take place publicly. Such group consumption includes drinking at bars, smoking and eating at parties, playing tennis and other sports, attending the theater, movies, or rock or symphonic concerts, eating at restaurants, attending school, praying and socializing at churches, visiting museums, working in teams and other groups, participating in strikes and other trade union activities, searching for marriage mates at social gatherings, caring for lawns visible to neighbors, decorating homes and offices, driving on one or the other side of roads, and being exposed to the publicity given to those who are punished for serious violations of laws.

Although this long list covers many aspects of modern life, it does not even exhaust activities with important public dimensions. Moreover, various kinds of private activities are also subject to strong social pressures. Advertising suggesting that Michael Jordan eats a particular breakfast cereal may induce many children and adults to eat this cereal so that they can vicariously be "closer" to this superb former basketball player.

Even though any help children provide their elderly parents may be directly known only to the children and parents, other families often learn about this either through gossip, or through observing the living condition of the parents. As a result, children have been subject to considerable social pressure to help their parents, especially in poorer societies without social security systems. In modern democracies, people vote privately, but the way they vote is often subject to enormous social influences through the preferences of others expressed in polls, discussions with friends, and from political campaigning.

Parents, schools, religions, governments, and other organizations and institutions mold the preferences of young people toward honesty, to respect elders, to pay or avoid payment of taxes, and toward other values and behavior. The internalization of such social norms of conduct into attitudes and preferences helps control many kinds of private behavior which are least subject to scrutiny by others.

These examples should make it clear that social influences on behavior are common and even pervasive. We are especially interested in the mutual interaction between social forces and market behavior, which we call "social markets." By markets we do not mean only ordinary market behavior, for we also consider implicit markets, such as marriage markets.

The analytical approach relies on the assumptions of utility maximization and equilibrium in the behavior of groups, which are the traditional foundations of rational choice analysis and the economic approach to behavior. This book shows how to incorporate social forces into this approach.

Part I derives various implications for the behavior of social influences; some of these differ substantially from the implications of conventional theories of choice. Part II discusses the effects of prices, altruism, laws, and other factors on the formation of social groups. It considers how individuals and families get sorted into different marriages, friendships, neighborhoods, income classes, schools, peer groups, churches, and consumer goods. Part III considers the dynamics of the formation of social influences through fads, fashions, and norms.

2. Prices in the Literature

The late James Coleman had a large influence on our interest in the relation between social forces and market behavior. This was partly through his fundamental treatise, *Foundations of Social Theory* (1990), in which he extensively analyzed social capital and other social influences on behavior. Even more important to us was the Seminar on Rational Choice in the Social Sciences that Coleman and Becker started in 1983 and ran together until Coleman's premature death in 1995. This interdisciplinary seminar had lively discussions of the relation between social forces and behavior.

We were surprised to discover, upon rereading Thorstein Veblen's influential *Theory of the Leisure Class* (1934), that he anticipated many of our results, although he does not make a systematic analysis. Veblen argues that social interactions are extremely important in modern economics; he particularly emphasizes behavior that conveys signals about one's wealth, that is, "conspicuous consumption," to use his famous phrase.

Thomas Schelling's *Micromotives and Macrobehavior* (1978) is a pioneering analysis of the influence of social groups on behavior. He has many insights concerning the dynamics of choices when individual preferences depend on group variables, such as the racial or income composition of neighborhoods. He shows the possibility of multiple equilibria, analyzes differences between stable and unstable equilibria, and considers determinants of "tipping" where neighborhoods undergo radical changes in composition by race, religion, income, and other characteristics.

The major contribution of our study to the literature is its systematic analysis of the effects of prices on market behavior where social interactions are important. Coleman, Veblen, and Schelling, for example, almost entirely ignore prices, whereas prices are a fundamental part of our analysis of the social multiplier on behavior, outcomes in marriage markets, the allocation of different groups to various neighborhoods, the rise and fall of fads and fashions, the escalation of product quality to separate leader from follower, and the distributions of incomes and status.

To be sure, prices are not important in some of the examples considered by others, such as Schelling's discussion of the wearing of protective masks in hockey, and of the social rules that govern when to applaud at concerts. However, prices are usually neglected when they are important, such as in marriage markets (see Gale and Shapley, 1962).

Without a systematic discussion of the effects of housing prices, Schelling could not determine whether there is "too much" or "too little" segregation in the housing market relative to the segregation that maximizes willingness to pay or relative to other criterion. The role of equilibrium prices in competitive housing markets is essential to our proof that the degree of neighborhood "segregation" of different social groups tends to be excessive compared with the level that maximizes aggregate willingness to pay (see Chapter 5, section 2).

Veblen's observation that beautiful objects often sell for much more than can be attributed to their beauty alone is a keen insight. But this cannot be proved without an analysis of how prices are affected by the interaction between the demand for beauty and the desire for social distinction. Our analysis in Chapter 6 of the demand for paintings by masters and for other objects proves this claim by relying heavily on the allocative role of prices in markets with social interactions.

In addition to the influence of Coleman, Veblen, and Schelling, we are indebted to a considerable literature by economists and sociologists on the relation between social interaction and individual choices. Theorists have been devising analytical techniques and trying to measure these relations. For example, the term "social capital" was apparently introduced by Loury (1977) and popularized by Coleman (1990). Other important work includes Hirsch (1976), which greatly influenced Frank (1985, 1999); Benabou (1996a, b); Glaeser, Sacerdote, and Scheinkman (1996); Brock and Durlauf (1995); Brenner (1983); and Weiss and Fershtman (1998).

Social Forces, Preferences, and Complementarity

1. Introduction

Economists usually assume that utility functions depend either directly on the goods and services consumed, or on household commodities produced with time and purchased goods and services. Social forces are either ignored or left to lurk in the background as part of the general environment. In this approach, changes in social forces would "shift" utility functions because they change the environment.

This approach is adequate for dealing with many kinds of behavior when the social environment is stable. However, it cannot analyze behavior that aims to change this environment, as when a family moves because it believes a different neighborhood would be better for its children. Moreover, it says little about how exogenous changes in the social environment alter behavior, and nothing about how the aggregation of all behavior itself determines the social environment.

The approach we take treats the social environment as arguments, along with goods and services, in a stable extended utility function. This provides a direct way to analyze how changes in this environment affect choices and behavior by changing the utilities of goods. Moreover, and perhaps even more important, it also provides a natural way to analyze how the social environment itself gets determined by the interaction of individuals.

Consider the utility function

(2.1) $U = U(x, y; S),$

where x and y are goods and services of all kinds, which we will refer to simply as goods. The variable S represents social influences on utility through stocks of "social capital." In the usual approach, utility depends directly on x and y, as in $V = V(x, y)$, so that changes in S would then shift the whole V function.

In equation (2.1), changes in social capital do not shift the utility function, but rather raise or lower the level of utility within the stable function, U. Moreover, even exogenous changes in S would affect behavior if these changes raise or lower marginal utilities of different goods. The utility from drugs, crime, going bowling, owning a Rolex watch, voting Democratic, dressing informally at work, or keeping a neat lawn depends on whether friends and neighbors take drugs, commit crimes, go bowling, own Rolex watches, vote Democratic, dress informally, or keep their lawns neat.

The fundamental assumption in analyzing the influence of social capital, S, on closely related behavior, x, is that S and x are *complements,* so that an increase in S raises the marginal utility from x, even when the increase in social capital itself lowers utility. Such complementarity between S and x means that an increase in S raises demand for x. For example, I would be more likely to vote Democratic, wear a tie at work, or buy a new car if my friends vote that way, wear ties, and have new cars.

Very strong complementarities is the technical way to incorporate into a utility-maximizing framework the claim that social forces have tyrannical power over individual behavior, that individuals are "forced" to conform to social norms, that culture is dominant, and other powerful effects of social structure on behavior commonly emphasized by sociologists and anthropologists. Strong complementarities help us understand why writers who highlight culture and social structure tend to downgrade the importance of individual choice, since strong complementarities between social capital and individual behavior appear to leave little room for individual choice.

Although at one level there is much validity to these claims, at a more fundamental level social capital changes the focus rather than reduces the importance of individual choice. If peer pressure and other forms of social capital have enormous power over choices, it becomes much more important to make wise decisions in selecting peers and other determinants of such capital. We treat the formation of social capital in Part II.

Even if social capital, S, severely constrains choices because of strong complementarities between S and various goods, these complementarities themselves have interesting implications for behavior. When complementarities are strong, they can destabilize the market for goods, create multiple equilibria, induce large responses in quantities to shifts in prices and other parameters, and cause other unusual behavior patterns. We will discuss some of these shortly.

For some purposes, it may be more enlightening to assume that goods and social capital do not directly enter utility functions, but rather are inputs into household functions that produce commodities, Z, the arguments of utility functions. From this perspective, equation (2.1) is a reduced form obtained after using household production functions to substitute x, y, and S for Z in the utility function. This interpretation allows us to consider the complementarity between social capital and consumption in equation (2.1) as reflecting a technological relation rather than a true preference or taste.

Take the convention of driving on the right-hand side of the road. People do not intrinsically care much about which side they drive on, but they do want very much to drive on the same side as everyone else. Therefore, if S refers to the side of the road others are driving on, and x to the side I drive on, S and x are very strong complements in producing the output "driving effectively to reach a destination." It is this produced output that enters utility functions. Still, although a production relation may be the source of these strong complementarities, it is legitimate to consider the reduced form where S and x directly enter the utility function.

More or less the same argument applies to complementarities produced by information linkages. A person may copy the choices made by others because he feels they have superior information (see Bikhchandani, Hirshleifer, and Welch, 1992). For example, he may go to popular restaurants because he believes that people in the "know" patronize restaurants that have good food and a pleasant atmosphere. In such cases, private information revealed by the behavior of others is the source of the strong complementarity between what they do and what I want to do. But the informational linkages that are the source of this complementarity can also usually be substituted to obtain utility functions that directly depend on social interactions.

Many economists do not believe that social structure and other social interactions have strong direct effects on preferences. They believe that informational and technological linkages are the source of most interactions between what others do and what I do. Unquestionably some are due to informational and technological linkages, but many important interactions are due to other considerations.

The desires for prestige and to conform are important in their own right, even when they do not provide information or technical advantages. For example, Veblen (1934) is surely right that conspicuous consumption is often motivated by the desire to appear wealthy to others, but the prestige from being considered wealthy often has little to do with technological and informational complementarities.

Most of the time, this book assumes that social capital directly enters preferences and is a complement in preferences with various goods. However, the discussion is usually also applicable when complementarities between this capital and goods are due to technological or informational linkages. We distinguish the source of the complementarity when it is important to do so.

2. Social Interactions and Demand

Assume for the present that each person takes S as exogenous to his own choices, although the collective choices by everyone may help determine S. Then a person would maximize the utility function in equation (2.1), subject to a given value of $S = S_0$ and his budget constraint

$$(2.2) \qquad p_x x + y = I,$$

where y is the numeraire and I is income. Given the usual assumptions about quasi-concavity of the utility function, the first-order maximizing conditions imply that an exogenous increase in S raises the demand for x if it raises the marginal utility of x relative to the (price) adjusted marginal utility of y; that is,

$$(2.3) \qquad \frac{dx}{dS} = \frac{p_x U_{yS} - U_{xS}}{D > 0} \qquad \text{if } U_{xS} > p_x U_{yS},$$

since $D < 0$ by the second-order conditions.

Notice that given the second derivatives in equation (2.3), the effect of changes in social capital on choices does not depend on whether additional social capital raises or lowers utility—the sign of U_S. It is not possible to determine the sign of the utility effect of greater peer pressure merely from how one's peers' consumption affects one's own behavior. For example, a teenager may take drugs more frequently because his peers do even when increases in their drug use lowers his utility.

Obviously, however, people would like to take actions and make choices that help them avoid peer pressure and other social capital that lowers their utility—perhaps that should be called negative capital. Similarly, they would be attracted to actions that raise the level of capital with positive utility to them. In this way, the sign of the effects on utility of different kinds of social capital becomes crucial in determining choices of friends, neighbors, schools and churches, and different commodities, and also decisions to migrate to other regions and countries. In turn, these choices determine the composition of neighborhoods, schools, and other groupings. Part II analyzes the formation of different kinds of social capital induced by the effects of social capital on utility.

In this chapter, however, we concentrate on individual choices that do not significantly affect a person's stocks of social capital. But to get much further with the analysis, it is necessary to analyze how the aggregate of all choices by members of the same social group influences the formation of their social capital. This chapter concentrates on perhaps the simplest example, where social capital equals the aggregate consumption of a good by members of the same social group. The group is assumed to be sufficiently large that changes in the consumption of that good by any one member have a negligible effect on the social capital stock and hence on the behavior of other members.

That is, the stock, S, equals the average of the x's chosen by all members of the same social group:

$$(2.4) \qquad S = X = \frac{1}{N} \sum x^j \qquad \text{where the sum is over } j \in G$$

and where N is assumed to be large enough that changes in any x^j hardly affect S. A typical member of group G chooses x^j by maximizing his utility, subject to his budget constraint and to a given value of S from equation (2.4).

The result of this maximization is a demand function for each x^j:

$$(2.5) \qquad x^j = d^j(e^j, p, S = X), \qquad \text{where } j = 1, 2, \ldots, N.$$

The variable e^j is an idiosyncratic one that affects j alone, such as her income or marital state; p is a variable that is common to all members of G, such as the price of x; and X is the level of social capital assumed by j in choosing her optimal x^j. By summing over all the x^j, we solve for the equilibrium level of X:

$$(2.6) \qquad X = \sum \frac{d^j(e^j, p, X)}{N} = \sum \frac{x^j}{N}, \quad \text{or} \quad X = F(e^i \ldots e^n, p).$$

Suppose social influences are very important, so that S and the x^j are strong complements. Then changes in an idiosyncratic variable like e^j are not likely to have much effect on the x^j since its strong complement, the social structure, would be virtually unchanged. This result is implied by the theory of rationing, which states that the elasticity of demand for a good is much smaller when a strong complement (or substitute) of this good is kept at a fixed quantity than when this complement also changes (see Deaton and Muelbauer, 1980, p. 109).

This is one sense in which individuals do not have much freedom to choose when social influences are powerful. For example, a rise in a family's income may not greatly affect its number of children or likelihood of divorce if the incomes of families in its social group have not changed, and if fertility and divorce choices are closely affected by fertility and divorce rates of families in this group.

Each individual choice alone still does not matter much when a variable common to all members of the group changes, such as the market prices of goods. But the sum of their choices then matters a great deal. For although each response to a common variable would have little effect on others, as with idiosyncratic changes, social capital multiplies the total effect due to the interactions among the individual effects. Taking the total derivative of equation (2.6),

$$(2.7) \qquad \frac{dS}{dp} = \frac{dX}{dp} = \frac{\sum dx^i/dp}{N} = \frac{\sum \partial x^i/\partial p}{N} + \frac{\sum (\partial x^i/\partial S)/(dS/dp)}{N},$$

or

(2.8)
$$\frac{dS}{dp} = \frac{\frac{1}{N}\sum \partial x^y / \partial p}{1 - m},$$

where $m = (1/N)\Sigma(\partial x^j/\partial S) > 0$.

The numerator in equation (2.8) is simply the average change of individual demands, which may be small when complementarities with social capital are strong. But complementarity between social capital and the demand for goods magnifies the aggregate effect of changes in variables that affect all members of the group. For as each member, say, increases her demand for x, that stimulates the demands of other members a little because of the group complementarity. This is why the numerator is divided by $1 - m$, a term less than one. The coefficient m, the "social multiplier," is determined from equation (2.3).

Since social conformity and other social interactions make the denominator small, there could be a very large response to changes in common variables even when there is only a small response to idiosyncratic variables. For example, a change in the income of one family alone may have only a small effect on its fertility rate, but changes in all families' incomes could have a huge effect. This could explain why declines in fertility over time caused by economic growth have generally been much greater than fertility differences between families at a moment in time. Similarly, changes in prices, advertising, and other variables that impact most members of a peer group may have very large effects on behavior.

A more extended example is the hostility to divorce that prevailed in Western countries for hundreds of years, and continued during the first half of the twentieth century. Even when couples were unhappily married, marital breakups in the past were discouraged by social hostility to divorce as well as by financial and other dependence on one's spouse.

During the late 1950s, many married women began to work, birth rates fell rapidly, the pill improved contraceptive effectiveness, and economies shifted from manufacturing toward services. As a result, more unhappily married men and women took the plunge and divorced. Dissolution rates increased slowly at first because the social forces against divorce were still powerful. But the hostility to divorced persons diminished as divorces increased, and "investments" in marriage also declined as couples anticipated a greater likelihood of breaking up (see Drewianka, 1999). In addition, legislatures were lobbied to change divorce laws to make breakups easier.

Five decades after this process started, family structures have changed remarkably. No longer is marriage considered inviolable, but rather divorce is expected with a reasonable likelihood. Alternative and conflicting lifestyles are increasingly viewed as equally "natural" and attractive, including not only stable heterosexual first marriages with children, but also second and third marriages of divorced persons, single parents, homosexual marriages, and group living. These changes in family-sexual patterns have picked up so much momentum that the long-run changes constitute a revolution in family mores and attitudes.

The social multiplier creates a cascading effect as members of a social group influence and reinforce one another's behavior. The informational cascades literature shows how early choices influence later choices because earlier choices reveal private information (see Bikhchandani, Hirshleifer, and Welch, 1992, p. 996). This cascade in sequential behavior is a special case of more general cascading due to social interactions and complementarity.

Social interactions make the social multiplier positive, but its precise value depends on the nature of the interaction and the degree of complementarity. The social multiplier, and the likelihood of a large response to a common change, increases as the influence of a group over its members rises.

For example, if each individual's demands are related to social capital in rigidly fixed proportions, then $x^j = w^j NS$, so that $m = (1/N)\Sigma(\partial x^j/\partial S) = 1$, where $\Sigma w^j = 1$. In this fixed-proportions case, the aggregate demand for x is indeterminate because of the overriding influence of peers on behavior. Demand by any member totally depends on the demands by other members of the same social group. Driving on the right- or left-hand side of the road is a good example. Driving on either side by everyone constitutes equally good equilibria, since if everyone else drives on the same side—either side will do—each person strongly wants to drive on that same side. Other examples include units of measure, such as the metrics system, and network standards, such as for VCRs and computing operating systems.

Fixed proportions imply that $m = 1$ because the demand for x by each j changes by the same percentage as S does. This is a very strong form of social interaction, but it is not the strongest form possible. The social multiplier could be above one because demand by a typical member could increase by a greater percentage than aggregate demand (see Chapter 9 for a discussion that uses $m > 1$ to understand fads).

3. Inequality

We have seen that complementarity between social capital and behavior increases conformity among members of the same group. However, such complementarity also magnifies differences among groups. To show this, assume a set of variables $p_1, \ldots, p_k$ that are common to all members of the same social group, but may differ between groups. Each person's behavior depends not only on the p but also on the choices (x^j) by other members of his group. Therefore the aggregate choices by all members of the same jth group can be written as:

$$(2.9) \qquad X^j = F(p_1^j, p_2^j, \ldots, p_k^j, X^j), \qquad j = 1, \ldots, G.$$

By taking a linear approximation to this function, ignoring the constant, and collecting terms we get, for this group,

$$(2.10) \qquad X^j = \frac{\sum b_i^j p_i^j}{1 - m^j}, \qquad j = 1, \ldots, G.$$

Glaeser, Sacerdote, and Scheinkman (1996) show that inequality in crime rates across U.S. cities appears to have a large social neighborhood component, too large for the inequality to be attributed to differences across cities in average incomes, education, age, and other variables. Social interactions also help explain the inequality in unemployment rates among Chicago census tracts (see Topa, 1996).

4. The Interaction of Habits and Social Capital

The analysis of complementarities in this chapter shows that social influences on behavior may cause multiple equilibria because each person's behavior depends on the behavior of others. An obvious example is whether cars drive on the left- or right-hand side of the road. Either side is equally good, as long as everybody drives on the same side.

But countries do not bounce from one side of a road to the other depending on the whims and inclinations of drivers—they stick to the side used in the past. The side of the road used and other conventions are seldom changed, partly because people build up habits and reflexes from past behavior. The United States stays with feet, miles, pounds, ounces, and so on even though the rest of the world mainly uses the much more efficient metric system, because Americans are habituated to this absurd system of weights and measures. The English and Japanese continue to drive on the left-hand side of the road, even though a switch to the right-hand side would make driving easier when visiting other nations, because a switch would destroy valuable habits and physical capital.

This section deals with interactions between habits and social forces like peer pressure and tradition. Habitual behavior encourages a continuation of past behavior. For example, a person is more likely to smoke, become a vegetarian, or use the Fahrenheit system if she has already engaged in these activities for a while. As Shakespeare said, "Use doth breed a habit." An *addiction* requires strong enough reinforcement from past behavior to cause unstable behavior (for this definition and further discussion see Becker, 1996, and Becker and Murphy, 1988). Habits depend on the behavior of past "selves," while social interactions depend on the behavior of other selves.

A simple way to analyze habitual behavior is through habit capital

$$(2.11) \qquad U^j = U(x^j, y^j, S^j, H^j),$$

where H^j is j's habit capital and S^j is j's social capital. If x is habitual, an increase in past consumption of x by j would increase H^j. Whether this would raise the present consumption of x by forward-looking individuals depends on the effect of H on both present marginal utilities of x and future stocks of H.

To see the effect on x of the joint action of H and S, consider a particular time-separable version of the utility function in equation (2.11):

$$(2.12) \qquad U^j(t) = v^j\{x^j(t) - [a\delta H^j(t) + bS(t)]\} + g^j[y^j(t)], \qquad \text{all } j \text{ in } G,$$

where v and g are concave, $a > 0$ is a parameter that measures how habitual is the consumption of x, δ is the common depreciation rate on past consumption of x, and $b > 0$ measures how strong are the social pressures to consume x, where S simply equals the average of the current consumption of x by all members of j's social group. This is a *modified* Stone-Geary utility function, modified by fixing H and S in the short run but not in the long run.

If all j in each G are identical, changes in consumption between steady states in response to a *marginal utility compensated* change in price, or in response to a compensated change in another common variable, is

(2.13)
$$\frac{dx}{dp} = \frac{\lambda}{v''(1-a)(1-a-b)},$$

where λ is the assumed constant marginal utility of wealth (see Becker, 1996, p. 135).

As equation (2.13) shows, habits and social pressures—measured by a and b, respectively—do not affect the response to price and other common changes symmetrically because a person's consumption affects her future habit capital but not her future social capital. But the most significant implication of this equation is that both habit and peer pressure interact to magnify the long-run response to changes in price. The long-run response would be large even when both habits and social pressures have only moderate effects—if the combined effect $(a + b)$ is large. The combined effect is more powerful than the sum of the separate effects because habitual and social behavior reinforce each other.

Many addictions—including smoking, drinking, and drug use—usually begin during teenage years when peer pressure is very strong. Perhaps smoking becomes highly addictive because of powerful peer pressures.

If $a + b > 1$, habit and peer effects are sufficiently strong to destabilize steady states: consumption would either explode toward higher values or contract toward zero. Goods with such unstable steady states fit the definition given above of addictive goods. However, if peer pressure is powerful—if b is large—goods can be "addictive" without a large a, or without strong reinforcement from past consumption, the usual definition of an "addiction." Moreover, goods with moderately strong social pressures and moderately strong reinforcement from past consumption are addictive if their combined effect is large enough (if $a + b > 1$).

5. Two Examples

Religion

Religions have been enormously popular throughout history, in part because they provide a set of doctrines and beliefs that help people face adversities and the unknown, especially eventual death. Nevertheless, many religious doctrines, including those about the afterlife, heaven and hell, Jesus being the son of God, and Muhammad being the last prophet, must be accepted on faith since they are not subject to proof or disproof.

Group prayer is a way to use social interactions to strengthen beliefs in the religious doctrines that must be accepted on faith. Christianity, Islam, Judaism, and many other religions hold group religious services in special temples, churches, mosques, and synagogues. Orthodox Judaism requires at least ten men to have a religious service. The doubts a person may have about various doctrines, such as the existence of an afterlife, presumably are reduced by observing others who appear to believe fervently. An increase in the number of persons who appear to have faith in particular doctrines would raise the willingness of others to accept the doctrines on faith.

The importance of such group influences suggests that the analyses of social interactions in this chapter might be particularly applicable to religions. The evidence on beliefs and religious affiliation is clearly consistent with strong complementarity among beliefs. If the relevant groups refer to neighborhoods, towns, cities, and even countries, beliefs tend to be homogeneous within peer groups but heterogeneous between peer groups. For example, the populations of most countries are either Catholic, Protestant, Muslim, Hindu, Buddhist, or nonbelievers, although exceptions like the United States have sizable minority religions as well as majority religions.

As implied by this analysis, there is a large inequality among countries in the strength of religious beliefs. Nominally Protestant Scandinavia and the former East Germany show little interest in religion, whereas Ireland and the United States display very high religiosity. Social interactions may be one important reason for these differences. The discussion in section 3 shows that the social multiplier would magnify small "incidental" variations in religiosity between countries, or small differences in religious parameters, into large differences in actual religiosity between countries.

Small changes over time in the attractiveness of different religions would also be magnified by social interactions into large changes over time in religious affiliations. For example, the proportion of Americans who attend church, believe in the existence of God and an afterlife, and have other religious beliefs apparently did not change very much during the twentieth century (see Iannaccone, 1998). Yet religion affiliation changed enormously: Baptists and other fundamentalist religions grew rapidly, while Methodist and other mainline Protestant sects decreased significantly.

Religion recovered quickly in Russia and some other countries in

Eastern Europe and Central Asia after the fall of communism, even though their former governments had tried for decades to suppress religion. However, inequality in religiosity among these countries also grew: religion has made little headway in the former East Germany, in Hungary, and in some of the other ex-communist countries (see Greeley, 1994).

Producers generally prefer to be monopolists since demand for their products increases when substitutes are not available. However, the gain from reduced competition is even greater in social markets because the social multiplier links the demand of different "customers." Perhaps this helps explain why religions have fought especially hard for a preferential position, and have used political clout to impose onerous burdens on competitors. These burdens include state subsidies to favored religions, legal restrictions on the rights of minority religions to recruit members, and laws that designate the holy days of favored religions as state holidays.

Religions often even include the inferiority of competing religions in their doctrines, and may impose major penalties on members who deviate from these precepts. For example, Muslim women can be killed for marrying non-Muslim men who do not convert to Islam. Religions are especially hard on adherents to new ("heretical") offshoot religions, as seen from the ferocious hostility of Islam to Bahaism and the opposition of mainline Protestant religions to Jehovah's Witnesses, Scientology, and Mormons, especially when Mormons advocated polygamy.

Fertility

Birth rates often change sharply over short stretches of time. For example, Spain and Italy have total fertility rates that are far below replacement levels, at about 1.2, although a few decades ago they had among the highest birth rates in Western Europe. In a mere thirty years, fertility in Hong Kong, Korea, and Taiwan dropped from very high levels to below replacement levels. In the 1960s birth rates among French Catholic Canadians were among the highest in Canada, whereas they have now dropped to about the Canadian average (see Balakrishnan, Lapierre-Adamczyk, and Krotki, 1993).

Rapid declines in fertility are usually explained by economic growth, the growing education of women, and the interaction between the quantity and quality of children (see Becker, 1991). These variables are adequate to explain many changes in fertility, but they cannot fully explain the patterns in Western Europe and elsewhere. For example, Italy and Spain are poorer and less educated than France and Germany, but they have lower fertility rates. French Canadians have lower incomes and education than the rest of Canada.

The explanation for these and other fertility changes is helped by recognizing that the number and education of children are affected by the behavior of friends, peers, and neighbors. Then births within a group could respond sharply to small changes in explanatory variables because the social multiplier magnifies responses of the members of the same social group.

An interesting study examined the onset of rapid fertility declines in many developing countries after 1960 (see Bongarts and Watkins, 1996). The authors find that increases in incomes and education reduce fertility from high predevelopment levels, but that these variables do not fully explain the actual declines. Holding constant income and education, fertility begins to decline earlier if it has already fallen in neighboring countries. They attribute this to social interactions across neighboring countries, although common changes in unobservable variables is a possible alternative explanation.

Are Choices "Rational" When Social Capital Is Important?

Individuals still "choose" their allocations of resources when social capital is important to their utility and strongly complementary with the demand for particular goods. But the discussion in this part of the book shows that choices are seriously constrained, since a person's actions are then partly determined by the actions of peers. Each member of a peer group may have little freedom to deviate from what other members are doing because his behavior would be mainly determined by their common culture, norms, and traditions.

Long before economists discovered the importance of social interactions, sociologists and anthropologists were emphasizing that social structure had tyranny over many kinds of behavior. One can appreciate the significance of the comment by the economist James Duesenberry (1960) on an early fertility paper of Becker that "economics is all about choice, while sociology is about why people have no choices." To some, the tyranny of culture and norms over behavior is so complete that a theory of individual rational "choices" is an oxymoron (see Sahlins, 1976).

Chapter 2 shows, however, that while members of the same peer group make similar choices because their behavior may be largely determined by their social capital, the behavior of different groups may be widely different. For example, residents of certain neighborhoods are under considerable social pressure to obey the law and help members of their community who are in trouble, while the prevailing social culture in some other neighborhoods is everyone for oneself, and to disobey the law if one can get away with it.

This implies that even when social structure and social capital have enormous power over behavior, people still greatly influence their behavior by, in effect, choosing their social capital. The tyranny of social structure over behavior does not then replace individual choice, but rather it shifts the crucial ones to selection of neighborhood, school, friends, marriage, occupation, and religion. The rich generally choose to live near other wealthy persons, academics are usually friendly with other academics, Catholics tend to marry other Catholics, criminals associate with other criminals, teenagers go to hangouts where they expect to find other teenagers, and so on for hundreds of other groups. The noted anthropologist Mary Douglas recognizes the importance of the choice of friends, spouse, and work when she states, "The real moment of choosing is . . . choice of comrades and way of life" (1983, p. 45).

When preferences sufficiently differ, everyone can choose whom to associate with. For example, peer preferences of teenagers and adults do not usually conflict, since teenagers want to be friends with other teenagers and adults prefer the company of other adults. Conflicts arise when preferences clash, so that the number of persons who want to join a particular group exceeds the number of places available. Many people want to be friendly with the rich and famous, to marry beautiful women or rich men, and to live near law-abiding and helpful families. But, alas, the number of friends of the rich, spouses of great beauties, or neighbors of good citizens is severely limited.

These examples indicate that similarity of preferences combined with heterogeneity of people is the underlying source of conflict in the formation of neighborhoods and other categories. The major analytical challenge created by these conflicts is to determine the composition of different social categories when limited numbers of persons can associate with more elite individuals. We believe that utility maximization and other parts of rational choice theory provide insight into how people are divided into different categories when some categories are in greater demand because they have more attractive members. That is, we hope to demonstrate that rational choice theory is not inconsistent with the importance of social structure, but rather is crucial in understanding how this structure gets determined.

Chapters 4–7 in Part II take the heterogeneity of the population as given, and assume that the population is divided into two groups, which we call "leaders" and "followers," "elites" and "others," or "highs" and "lows." Conflict arises because members of both the "higher" and the "lower" groups prefer various associations with star athletes, Nobel laureates, rich businessmen, better students, law-abiding families, fashion-setters, and other types of higher persons. These chapters mainly consider selection of marriage mates, neighborhoods, schools, churches, collectible items, and consumer goods.

Chapter 8 analyzes how individuals get into higher status categories, such as leaders and elites, by considering the determination of the distribution of incomes through lotteries and other risky activities. Leaders are usually richer and more successful than others (see Gladwell 2000 for a popular discussion of the importance of leaders).

However, this book does not try to weigh the various motives that induce most people to want to associate with elites by being in the same neighborhoods and other categories. Veblen emphasized that conspicuous consumption is motivated by a desire to project favorable, even if false, signals and images about whether a person is wealthy. Veblen believed that for wealth to have social significance, it "must be put in evidence, for esteem is awarded only on evidence" (1934, p. 36; for a rigorous formulation of a Veblen signaling model, see Bagwell and Bernheim, 1996).

He claimed that the desire to signal wealth had become more important as countries became wealthier, because the basic necessities of life were now more easily satisfied. The growth of the importance of cities also raised the need to signal wealth, due to the anonymity of city life (1934, pp. 86–89).

We agree with Veblen that the desire to be taken for one of the elites is a powerful motive, probably especially in richer and more urban societies, although sumptuary laws of the Middle Ages and earlier times prevented other classes from wearing the same clothing as nobility. However, we believe Veblen overemphasized the signaling of wealth relative to other reasons for associating with elites that have little to do with conspicuous consumption. People often receive considerable satisfaction from various contacts with elites, even when they do not pretend to be elites themselves. To take a simple example, collectors of autographs of successful athletes, politicians, Nobel laureates, and others do not try to signal that they are themselves famous athletes, politicians, and so on.

People get various pleasures from living in the same community, wearing similar clothes, and attending the same schools as elites and other leaders. We briefly discuss in Chapter 2 several motivations for this: a belief that elites have superior knowledge, insecurity about one's own tastes, invidious snobbery, personal satisfaction from consuming the same goods as leaders, and other psychological and sociological considerations.

Even Veblen recognized various exceptions to his emphasis on conspicuous consumption to convey signals about one's wealth. He admits that "prescriptive expensiveness is observable also in consumption that does not . . . become known to outsiders. . . . articles of clothing, some articles of food, kitchen utensils" (1934, p. 115). He lamely claims that *habits* of conspicuous consumption to signal wealth and status carry over to behavior that provides no signals (pp. 116–117).

Various cultural forces control the behavior of leaders as well as followers, perhaps because their common behavior is closely related to the actions of parents and earlier generations. These common forces cannot usually be greatly influenced by choosing different neighborhoods, friends, or other categories, aside perhaps from migrating to a very different culture. In the short run, such cultural forces may strikingly constrain the scope for individual "choices." But even behavior that may be largely constrained by culture in the short run is often highly sensitive to choices in the longer run.

This difference between short- and long-run effects is clearly seen in the strong stigma against divorce that prevailed in Western countries until a few decades ago. As we have seen, that stigma and norm discouraged divorce even by unhappily married couples, and ostracized the few women who dared to become "divorcees." However, the sharp growth in the labor force participation of married women combined with other forces induced a sustained rise in the breakup of families since the 1960s, which has largely eroded the stigma attached to divorce.

The "culture" in favor of stable heterosexual family life has virtually disappeared. Not only have divorces become common, but so too have births to unmarried women, acceptance of homosexuality, and other contradictions to the traditional norm about family life.

The rigidity of norms and culture in the short run and their plasticity in the long run is not unique to marriage, but applies to all norms and culture embedded in social markets that emerge from preferences and utility maximization. Chapter 2 has already shown this, but Part III provides a more systematic analysis of the dynamics of the formation and dissolution of culture and norms. The upshot of this discussion is that individual rational choices in a society with strong cultural influences is not an oxymoron, but rather that the interaction of choice and culture produces novel, important, and neglected behavior.

PART II

The Formation of Social Capital

CHAPTER 4

Sorting by Marriage

1. Conflict in Marriage Markets

Marriage is a good starting point for the analysis of the allocation of heterogeneous individuals to different groups. With monogamy, the number of places in each marriage is strictly limited to two, although mistresses and boyfriends may complicate relationships, and divorce permits serial polygamy.

Moreover, for most persons, their choice of a spouse—or of spouses if polygamy or divorce is allowed—is one of their most far-reaching and significant decisions. Adults typically have more frequent and more intimate contact with their spouse than with anyone else, so that the preferences and attitudes of most couples become much more similar if they stay married for many years. Moreover, marital sortings have an enormous influence on the values, preferences, and skills of a couple's children. Therefore, the way adults sort into different marriages makes a tremendous difference to the distribution of the characteristics of children from different families.

Participants in "marriage markets," including those who return after a divorce, differ greatly by income, education, age, health, appearance, personality, race, religion, ethnicity, family background, and other characteristics. A major goal of an analysis of marriage is to determine how these participants get sorted into different marriages. A marriage market equilibrium is a sorting of men and women into marriages, or to remaining single, whereby no two persons can expect to be made better off by changing mates and marrying each other instead.

One approach to marital sorting and marital equilibrium assumes that participants differ greatly in their rankings of other participants, that these differences are *given and fixed,* and that they create irreducible conflicts among participants in whom they want to marry (see especially Gale and Shapley, 1962, and Roth and Sotomayor, 1990). For example, A may want to marry B, who prefers marriage to C, who in turn may want to marry A. In these cases, a sorting equilibria is not usually unique, for it depends on who does the proposing and other aspects of the algorithm used to express preferences.

Obviously, there are considerable differences in many marital preferences since, for example, Catholics may prefer to marry Catholics, blacks to marry blacks, and tall people to marry tall people. However, strong differences of this type may simply decompose the overall marriage market into various homogeneous submarkets, where participants in each submarket, such as the white or black submarket, marry others in the same submarket.

Within each submarket, there may be considerable agreement and little conflict ex ante about how to rank participants who differ greatly in earnings and other characteristics. They may all more or less agree ex ante that richer, more educated, handsomer, wiser, kinder, more reliable, or funnier persons are more desirable. Of course, as participants look for mates, disagreement grows because they "fall in love" with different persons whom they meet. Hence they may *come* to differ greatly in whom they want to marry, despite their ex-ante agreement on the ranking of different participants.

As a first approximation to a fuller analysis, we assume that all men and women in each submarket agree, ex ante, on the ranking of the characteristics of the N women and K men in the same submarket, W_1, ..., W_n, M_1, ..., M_k. The highest subscripts indicate the highest rankings, so that women prefer M_j to M_i, and men prefer W_j to W_i, if $j > i$. This agreement can be stated formally by assuming marital output, Z, is the same function of M and W for all marriages, while M and W are ordered numbers, and this function has the following properties:

(4.1) $$Z = Z(M, W), \quad \text{with} \quad \frac{\partial Z}{\partial M} > 0 \quad \text{and} \quad \frac{\partial Z}{\partial W} > 0.$$

We have emphasized what may seem paradoxical: that with sufficiently sharp disagreement over rankings of potential mates, conflict in the marriage market may not be very great, since the market may decompose into distinct and independent marital submarkets. Indeed, the fundamental conflict is much greater not when, say, Catholics greatly prefer marrying other Catholics and Protestants prefer Protestants, but when there is considerable agreement over the ranking of potential mates.

Clearly, all men who prefer W_n to the other women would like to marry her, other things the same. However, since only one man can do so, a market process must decide whom she marries. Similarly, other things the same, all women may want to marry M_k, but only one woman can do so. How preferences determine the equilibrium sorting of marriages depends crucially on the place of love, on the role of prices and bidding in marriage markets, including bride prices and dowries in marriage markets, and on properties of the output function Z that may go far beyond the properties of first derivatives.

2. Equilibrium Sorting with Flexible Prices

We start out with the assumption that marital output, Z, is a fully divisible single good, that the number of women in the market, N, equals the number of men, K, that they all marry, and that the sum of the marital incomes of husbands and wives exhausts total output:

$$(4.2) \qquad Z(M_i, W_j) = Z_{ij} = I_i^m + I_j^w,$$

where I^m and I^w refer to the incomes of men and women. In this situation, each person's utility function is assumed to depend only on his or her own marital income, and the marriage market allows the M_i and W_j to bid for different spouses by offering a larger or smaller share of the output they would produce together.

An equilibrium sorting under these conditions has a set of incomes for all W and M, I_i^{*w} and I_i^{*m}, and an equilibrium allocation of all W and M to one member of the opposite sex (polygamy is considered in Becker, 1991), such that no two persons not married to each other in the equilibrium sorting could marry and make each better off. It follows that for any M_i and W_j not married to each other in the equilibrium sorting,

$$(4.3) \qquad I_i^{*m} I_j^{*w} > Z_{ij}$$

The characteristics of an equilibrium sorting given by equations (4.2) and (4.3), and whether it is unique, depends on properties of the cross derivative of the output function. In particular, it can be shown (see Becker, 1991; for an excellent exposition of equilibrium in such a marriage market, see Weiss and Willis, 1997) that there is perfect positive sorting—the "best" woman marries the "best" man, the next best women marries the next best man, and so on until the worst woman marries the worst man—if, and only if,

$$(4.4) \qquad \frac{\partial(\partial Z/\partial M)}{\partial W} = \frac{\partial^2 Z}{\partial M \partial W} > 0 \qquad \text{for all } M \text{ and } W.$$

A more general condition is that the Z function is super modular (see Milgrom and Roberts, 1990). Put differently, there is a unique equilibrium marital sorting with perfect segregation by quality if characteristics of men and women are complements in the production of marital output. By "segregation" we mean that the "best" of one sex is matched to the "best" of the other sex, the "next best" are also matched, and so on until the "worst" of each sex are matched.

Conversely, the "best" of one sex would be matched with the "worst" of the other if their characteristics are substitutes in the production of marital output; that is, if

$$(4.5) \qquad \frac{\partial^2 Z}{\partial M \partial W} < 0 \qquad \text{for all } M \text{ and } W.$$

If characteristics are everywhere substitutes, the unique equilibrium is integrating or "pooling," for it mixes together high and low qualities of men and women.

If characteristics of men and women are independent in production, then

$$(4.6) \qquad \frac{\partial^2 Z}{\partial M \partial W} = 0 \qquad \text{for all } M \text{ and } W.$$

Marriage then has no effect on output, and all sortings are equally good.

Equation (4.3) can be used to show that equilibrium incomes are not unique under the assumptions made so far. For example, given a set of values that satisfy equation (4.3), this equation and equation (4.2) continue to be satisfied if a constant is added to the incomes of all men and subtracted from the incomes of all women. Presumably, Nash or other kinds of bargaining in marriage help choose a particular set of equilibrium prices from the infinite set possible in this case (see McElroy and Horney, 1981, and Lundberg and Pollak, 1996, on bargaining in marriage).

The range of possible values is reduced with unequal numbers of men and women. Then some men or women must remain single, and incomes of single men (or women) set a floor to the equilibrium incomes of married men (or women). Moreover, the set of equilibrium incomes can be reduced to a unique set if there is sufficient continuity in the characteristics of participants (see Sattinger, 1975).

This theory of marriage markets shows how shifts in various parameters change equilibrium incomes. For example, increases in the number of women relative to men—perhaps due to male deaths during a major war—would lower incomes of women and raise those of men. Similarly, the decline in the relative number of women in Korea and other Asian nations due to the growth in recent years of sex-selected abortions (see Ichimura and Kim, 1996) should ultimately raise the demand for and incomes of women (see Grossbard-Shechtman, 1993). Empirical studies by Browning and Chiappori (1998) find that increases in the ratio of men to women tend to raise the share of marital output received by women.

There is a high degree of positive marital sorting in virtually all characteristics that have been measured, including education, IQ, family background, race, religion, age, and height. This implies that if marriage markets have flexible incomes, then most characteristics are complements in marriage—are super modular—given by a positive sign of the cross derivative in equation (4.4). Complementarity of most traits is eminently plausible, for mates of similar ages and education are more likely to have compatible interests, mates of the same religion can more readily accommodate their church attendance and beliefs in God, and similarly for many other characteristics.

The sharp segregation of marriages by various characteristics has major economic and social implications. Positive sorting increases inequality across marriages and, perhaps even more significantly, increases the inequality of investments in the human capital and values of the children of these marriages. In recent years, economists have followed sociologists by becoming very interested in the transmission of inequality from parents to children (see, for example, Becker, 1981,

1993; Solon, 1992; and Mulligan, 1997). However, they have emphasized parental characteristics, such as education and income, while paying little attention to positive sorting between parents.

Yet sorting on education, income, race, religion, and other characteristics in marriage is probably far more important in transmitting
inequality than capital market restrictions on investments in human
capital, neighborhood segregation, and the other variables usually emphasized. Kremer (1997) and Fernández and Rogerson (1999) use empirical evidence on the intergenerational transmission of inequality to
estimate the effects on inequality of shifting from the actual strong positive sorting of parents' characteristics to random or negative sorting of
these characteristics. Kremer does not find large effects, but his calcula-
tions have been criticized by Fernández and Rogerson.

We do not know of modern recommendations to force more random
mating of men and women to reduce inequality; in fact, until this century, many laws discouraged marriages across races, religions, and social classes. However, in his *Republic,* Plato strongly urged desegregation in marriage in order to reduce inequality and to obtain better
"mixtures":

> We will say to him who is born of good parents,—O my son, you
> ought to make such a marriage as wise men would approve. . . . al-
> ways to honour inferiors, and with them to form connexions;—
> this will be for the benefit of the city and of the families which are
> united . . . everyone is by nature prone to that which is likest to
> himself, and in this way the whole city becomes unequal in prop-
> erty and in disposition . . . the rich man shall not marry into the
> rich family, nor the powerful into the family of the powerful . . . we
> should try . . . to charm the spirits of men into believing the equa-
> bility of their children's disposition to be of more importance than
> equality of excessive fortune when they marry. (1953, pp. 340–
> 341)

3. Altruism and Love

It might appear that our assumption of competitive marriage markets
and flexible bidding biases the implications toward positive sorting of
men and women, since richer and better educated individuals can outbid others for the more preferred mates. But while they *could* outbid
others, they may not *want* to. Indeed if the characteristics of men and

women are substitutes in the production of marital incomes, the top men would be outbid by low men for the top women, and women with better characteristics would be outbid by women with worst characteristics for the top men. Indeed, with substitution, sorting would be perfectly negative on the relevant characteristics.

As this example indicates, competition and flexible incomes in marriage markets does not bias the outcomes toward positive sorting of the characteristics of husbands and wives. Indeed, price flexibility gives the sign of the second derivative of the marital output function a major influence over the nature of marital sortings, while other procedures for marriage sorting rely mainly only on the sign of *first* derivatives.

Only the first derivative is relevant when the marital shares are fixed rather than determined in the marriage market. For example, marital output may be family goods that must be jointly consumed, or religious and civil law may require marital output to be shared equally between husbands and wives, regardless of market forces. We consider a generalized version of such rules, where all husbands get the fraction ϕ of the output from their marriages, and wives get the fraction β:

$$(4.7) \qquad I_j^m = \phi Z(M_j, W_i), \quad \text{and} \quad I_i^w = \beta Z_{ij},$$

where $\phi + \beta$ adds up to a constant that could be greater, equal to, or less than one; for example, $\phi + \beta > 1$ if Z is a family good.

The maximum output in any possible marriage occurs when the top man and the top woman marry. Hence, since by equation (4.7), each man and each woman get a constant fraction of their marital output, the top man, M_k, and the top woman, W_n, would maximize their marital incomes by marrying each other. Since bidding is ruled out by the assumption of rigid shares, no one of lower quality can outbid them for the top man or woman, regardless of the second derivative of the output function. After the top man and woman choose each other, the next best men and women would marry each other since they each maximize their marital incomes that way, and no one can outbid them. The process continues until the least desirable man and woman marry each other.

The result is once again perfect segregation by quality, but note that we did not specify anything at all about the second derivative. Even if men and women are substitutes in the production of marriage output, so that total marital output is maximized with perfect negative sorting, men and women would sort positively if they always received a fixed, possibly unequal, share of their marriage output. By contrast, flexible prices in this case would overcome any tendency toward positive sorting by allowing low-quality men and women to outbid high-quality men and women for the top quality of the other sex.

Marriages with altruism or love are an important example of the sharing of output in a nonmarket way. Over the centuries, marriages based on love rather than on material rewards, convenience, or family alliances grew in importance as the individuals marrying, rather than their parents, began more frequently to choose their spouses. Moreover, companionate marriages became more common as husbands and wives began to spend much more time with each other than under traditional marriages (Posner, 1992). The importance of marrying for love increased as husbands and wives became more dependent on each other than on other family members for support during illness and bad times (Becker, 1991).

It would appear that love and altruism weaken the degree of positive sorting in marriage, since falling in love depends on many idiosyncratic factors that may not be closely related to characteristics, like income and education, that determine the production of marital output. The heiress who falls in love with her chauffeur and the business leader who falls in love with his assistant are often-repeated examples of the marital "mismatches" that love can create.

Although love clearly sometimes does transcend social and economic barriers, a closer analysis produces a paradox: positive sorting of "likes" may be even more important when men and women marry only when they are in love, that is, the growth of marriages based on love and altruism may have increased rather than decreased positive sorting by education, income, and similar characteristics, even when these characteristics of men and women are substitutes rather than complements in marital production.

To show how altruism affects marital sorting, we make a strong but reasonable assumption for the modern world that two people marry if, and only if, they are in love. After they marry, we assume they have separable utility functions with two terms: one depends on their own consumption, and the other altruistic part depends on their spouse's consumption:

$$(4.8) \qquad U_m = u(C_m) + a_w u(C_w),$$

(4.9)
$$U_w = v(C_w) + a_m v(C_m),$$

where C_m and C_w refer to the consumption of husbands and wives, a_w and a_m to the degree of their altruism, and u and v are increasing concave functions.

To highlight the importance of love, we start out with a strong degree of altruism: that mates get as much utility from their spouses' consumption as they get from their own consumption ($a_w = a_m = 1$). That is, mates fully agree on the allocation of resources between them.

To allow the second derivative of the output function to be a major determinant of marital sorting, we assume also that all marital output is private and divisible. For example, if u and v are linear with zero intercepts and unitary slopes,

(4.10)
$$U_m + U_w = 2(C_m + C_w) = 2Z_{mw}.$$

The combined utility of husbands and wives in this case does not equal total output, but it is *twice* total output because mutual altruism causes total marital output to be counted twice.

In the more general case with $a = 1$, the strong altruism in equations (4.8) and (4.9) implies that the spouse with the larger marital income will make gifts to his wife or her husband to raise his or her standard of living. If gifts can be transferred dollar for dollar, gifts would equalize the marginal utilities of the consumption of both spouses. Equations (4.8) and (4.9) then imply that regardless of any differences between the u and v utility functions, the person with the larger income always transfers enough resources to equalize the couple's consumptions.

That is, after the transfers induced by altruism,

(4.11)
$$C_m^* = C_w^* = \tfrac{1}{2}Z_{mw}, \quad \text{and}$$

(4.12)
$$U_m^* = 2u(\tfrac{1}{2}Z_{mw}), \quad \text{and} \quad U_w^* = 2v(\tfrac{1}{2}Z_{mw}),$$

which generalize equation (4.10).

It might appear that the sorting induced by love would still be heavily influenced by the sign of the second derivative of the marital output function. For if, say, characteristics of men and women are substitutes in production, a negative sorting equilibrium would still seem to gain the productivity advantages from a negative sorting as well as advantages from altruism.

This is plausible, but wrong. Strong altruism largely eliminates the relevance of the second derivative, and has effects on the equilibrium sorting similar to those of family goods and other factors that rigidly determine the distribution of output. This unintuitive result holds because people can influence whom they fall in love with and marry.

To show how love and altruism influence sorting, assume plausibly that people only fall in love through dating and other contacts. Love is an acquired taste, as it were, acquired through experience with other persons. Suppose that the probability of falling in love depends neither on one's own nor on other persons' characteristics that determine marital output. Although persons of similar education and religion are generally *more* likely to fall in love, we make this independence assumption to avoid biasing the discussion toward positive sorting.

Since falling in love requires dating and other search, there might be an advantage in searching for potential mates among particular groups. For example, if the characteristics of men and women are substitutes in production, high-quality men and women would seem to be better off by searching among low-quality women and men.

Yet this seemingly plausible inference is invalid, and high-quality men and women would search for mates among one another, even with substitution in production. With substitution, high-quality men and women would maximize incomes by falling in love with and marrying low-quality mates. However, since their income would tend to exceed that of low-quality mates, love and altruism would induce them to make gifts to their mates. These gifts reduce their own consumption below their incomes.

Equation (4.12) shows that altruism and gift-giving cause equilibrium utilities to depend not on incomes, as with selfish persons, but on total marital output. Therefore, men and women want to find marriages that maximize not their incomes, but total marital output. This is the same conclusion as with rigid marital shares, and has similar implications.

Consider search by the top men and women. Each would prefer to search among high-quality persons of the opposite sex, for marriage between the top men and women would maximize their marital output. Hence, such marriages maximize their equilibrium utility, if they are in love when they marry. Top people do not find it harder to fall in love by searching among one another since by assumption they are as likely to fall in love with one another as with members of lower groups. Top families, in fact, do expedite such search by their children through living in socially segregated neighborhoods and thereby making sure their offspring attend the same schools, churches, and parties (see Chapter 5).

Lower-quality men and women also prefer to be in love with and marry top persons, for equilibrium utilities after the gifts they would likely receive are higher when the characteristics of spouses who love them are better. This explains the age-old advice of mothers to their daughters: "If you are going to fall in love, you might as well fall in love with a rich man."

However, lower-quality persons may not be able to break into the high-quality market since high-quality persons do not want low-quality mates. If the latter cannot enter the more desirable high-quality market, low-quality persons have to confine their search to lower-quality mates. As a result, the vast majority of persons generally end up falling in love with and marrying within their own "class."

Consequently, where love and altruism are necessary conditions of marriage, the equilibrium sorting tends to be strongly positive, regardless of whether male and female characteristics are substitutes or complements in production. To be sure, however, a chess game goes on between high-quality persons, who try to avoid getting entangled with lower-quality persons of the opposite sex, and the latter, who want to find mates among the elites. Some charming persons of both sexes overcome the odds, and enter into love marriages with persons who have vastly superior market opportunities. But as we shall see, they may have trouble staying married.

Negative sorting maximizes total marital output when the characteristics of men and women are substitutes in production. Then lower-quality persons would prefer marriage to higher-quality mates even without gifts because their marital incomes would be higher with a negative sorting. To induce higher-quality persons to marry them, they might offer to sign prenuptial agreements and make other promises not to accept gifts after marriage.

But these promises will not be effective if everyone who marries is in love. For if high-quality spouses love their low-quality mates, they *want* to give them gifts in order to raise their consumption to more equal levels. Hence they would *not* respect any prenuptial agreements. They would violate them if they got married, and their mates would be happy to benefit from these violations ex post.

Therefore, even very self-denying prenuptial agreements offered by low-quality persons would not entice high-quality persons to search among lower-quality persons. For they still want to avoid falling in love with and marrying low-quality persons.

Instead of assuming that all persons love their spouses as much as themselves, a more reasonable assumption is that they love themselves more than they love their spouses. That is, the coefficients a_w and a_m in equations (4.8) and (4.9) are generally <1, perhaps much less. As these coefficients approach zero, the analysis of sorting approaches that among selfish participants in section 2. The nature of the sorting would then be determined by the sign of the second derivative of the marital output function.

The higher the altruism coefficients, the less important is the sign of the second derivative in determining the equilibrium sorting, and the more likely this sorting is strongly positive—only because of altruism if the cross derivative in the output function is negative. Still, altruism has important implications for behavior even when individuals considerably prefer their own utility to their spouses'.

Suppose the equilibrium sorting is perfectly positive, and assume that because of the strong positive sorting, equilibrium utilities of spouses are similar. Then if both a_w and a_m are significantly <1, neither spouse will make any altruistic transfers to the other—they only might trade household time for money. As a result, a redistribution of incomes within the range set by the magnitude of their altruism coefficients that does not induce any transfers between spouses would obviously have no effect on giving to each other, since there is none.

The empirical evidence of Browning and Chiappori (1998) and Grossbard-Shechtman (1993) indicates that love does not fully determine consumption within marriages since the sharing of resources between spouses is affected by the sex ratio in the community and other variables. There is also evidence that whether governments make transfer payments to husbands or wives affects how they are spent (see the summary of this evidence in Lundberg and Pollak, 1996).

However, even in these cases, altruism would have had a major effect on the marriage market if the altruism coefficients are sizable enough to produce a strong positive sorting of the characteristics of spouses when there would be a negative sorting without any altruism. Moreover, the utility of married men and women might still depend significantly on the utilities of their spouses, so that a large fall in these utilities would greatly lower their own welfare. Large enough falls in the utilities of spouses—perhaps due to major illness—would induce positive transfers to these spouses as long as the altruism coefficients are positive (see Fernandes, 1999, for a derivation of various implications of partial altruism).

The lesson of this discussion is that the importance of altruism cannot be assessed simply from the extent of giving, or from how giving responds to a redistribution of resources between spouses, or between parents and children, which is the way most of the literature tries to test for altruism (see, for example, Altonji, Hayashi, and Kotlikoff, 1997). In the case just discussed, altruism may profoundly change the nature of the marital sorting even though most marriages might have minor or no transfers. A further implication discussed in the next section relates to the effects of altruism on which marriages are more likely to break up.

4. Falling out of Love

Of course, as the expression "marry in haste, repent at leisure" makes clear, even the deepest and most passionate love often does not last. Love can turn to loathing, disdain, and sometimes to ferocious hatred as couples learn more about each other after they live together and as they encounter the many difficulties and frictions of life. Better knowledge of factors that cause couples to fall out of love would be enormously valuable in understanding the determinants of divorce and marital dissolution.

We address an easier question. If different couples are equally likely to fall out of love, which ones are more likely to dissolve their marriages? To answer this in the most important case, suppose that positive sorting is efficient because the cross derivative of the marital output function is positive. However, some couples are negatively sorted because they fell in love despite the best efforts of high-quality persons to search only in markets occupied mainly by other high-quality individuals.

"Mismatched" couples probably more easily fall out of love than well-matched couples. But even if mismatched couples do not more easily fall out of love, they are more likely than matched couples to dissolve their marriages when their love wanes—assuming that positive sorting is more efficient. For they only married against their "interests" because they fell in love. When proposing for the first time to Elizabeth Bennett in Jane Austen's *Pride and Prejudice*, Darcy arrogantly tells her that their marriage of unequals would obviously be against his interests, but he cannot help himself because he was unfortunate enough to fall in love with her.

Once love wanes, there are smaller gains to hold a marriage together in mismatched than in well-matched couples. Consequently, assuming they were equally in love initially, mismatched couples are more likely to break up than well-matched couples for any given decline in their love. Moreover, the amount of decline in love that would cause a breakup would be smaller in mismatched than in well-matched couples. If divorce had been accepted in eighteenth-century England, Darcy surely would have terminated his marriage to Elizabeth if they had fallen even moderately out of love.

There is in fact substantial evidence that couples of different religions, races, ethnicities, family backgrounds, and other characteristics are much more likely to divorce than couples with similar characteristics. The interpretation by Becker, Landes, and Michael (1977) is that "mismatched" couples gain the least from marriage since they were unlucky searchers in marriage market environments with significant economic advantages from positive sorting.

In our analysis of love marriages, it is also true that mismatched couples are "unlucky" to fall in love when positive sorting is optimal. However, mismatched couples who remain in love may do very well in utility terms, even though the higher-quality men or women might have done much better if they had fallen equally in love with more appropriate mates. But higher-quality mismatched spouses who fall out of love during their marriage do worse than higher-quality well-matched spouses, and they have more incentive to look for new spouses.

5. Do Marriage Markets Induce Optimal Investments in Human Capital?

This section discusses whether equilibrium marital sortings are Pareto efficient. We discuss both whether the equilibrium sorting is efficient, given the characteristics of men and women in the marriage market, and also whether men and women make efficient investments in their human capital to change their characteristics.

If all marital output is private, with full information about all traits, and if marital shares of men and women are fully determined by competition in the marriage market, then it is easy to show that the equilibrium sorting is efficient. A positive sorting maximizes aggregate marital output when the second derivative is positive, a negative sorting maximizes output when this derivative is negative, and so on (see the proof in Becker, 1981, 1993).

The more difficult question is whether there are efficient incentives to invest in greater schooling, plastic surgery to improve appearance, better clothing, and other human capital to marry a better person. Recall Darwin's (1859) famous claim that evolutionary advantage induced male peacock's tails to become excessively big to attract female peacocks. Darwin raised the important question of whether competition for mates induces overinvestment in advantageous characteristics of males and females.

Some economists, notably Robert Frank (1985, 1999), have picked up Darwin's argument and claim that the desire to gain a better position in the competition for incomes or spouses invariably leads to excessive investment in energy, time, and goods. These arguments seem plausible, but they have a major defect when marital and related prices not only assign individuals to each other but also determine the imputation of jointly produced outputs. With sufficiently flexible prices, investments to move up in the rankings of those eligible for marriage would be fully efficient. However, either too much or too little may be invested when prices are inflexible.

To show this, assume that the cost, but not the benefit, to single individuals of investing in different kinds of human capital to become more attractive in the marriage market is independent of the marital sorting, and also is independent of the distribution of incomes in different marriages. Rates of return on these investments are then fully determined by the higher incomes and utilities from having better characteristics. If these incomes and utilities are the result of competition and pricing in marriage markets, perhaps because all persons are selfish and all marital output is private, then investments in human capital that increase a person's marital productivity and rank are fully efficient. Since each person gets his or her marginal marital contribution, the marriage market would provide efficient investment signals, even when investments are made with an eye to move up the ranking in attractiveness.

Moreover, the investment incentives are efficient even though the addition of a constant to all male incomes and the subtraction of the same amount from all female incomes does not affect the equilibrium sorting. The incentive to invest remains efficient after such addition and subtraction because it does not affect the equilibrium income differences between males or females with different characteristics.

The conclusions about efficiency are quite different when men and women receive not their marginal product but a fixed share of marital output. Suppose that men receive a large share partly because they have more political and social power than women. In this case, men would gain a great deal from improving their characteristics because they would receive a large part of a bigger output by raising their rank in the distribution of male characteristics.

Under these conditions of high and fixed shares, men would tend to invest more in schooling and other human capital than is warranted by the *social* gain from these investments. However, women's incentives to invest in schooling and other characteristics are weaker when they receive a small and fixed share of marital output. Women would tend to invest less than is warranted by the social productivity of their investments.

More rigorously, when marital shares are rigidly fixed, as in equation (4.7), if one sex has locally excessive investment incentives the other has insufficient investment incentives, because their combined gain from investments would equal the total increase in marital outputs. If men in the past tended to overinvest in improving their human capital because they received excessive shares due to their greater power, women would have underinvested in their human capital.

A proof is straightforward (we owe this to Iván Werning). Let $I_m^*(m)$ and $I_w^*(w)$ be the equilibrium incomes of M and W, the matching function be $w = f(m)$, and $m = f^{-1}(w) = g(w)$. If men get the rigid share α, and women get $1 - \alpha$,

$$I_m^*(m) = \alpha Z[m, f(m)],$$

and

$$I_w^*(w) = (1 - \alpha)Z[g(w), w].$$

Take the total derivative

$$I_m^{*'}(m) = \alpha Z_m + \alpha Z_w f'(m),$$

and similarly for W. By further manipulation,

$$(4.13) \qquad I_m^{*\,\prime}(m) - Z_m = f'(m)[Z_w - I_w^{*\,\prime}].$$

The left-hand side gives the difference between the M's marginal income as they improve their characteristics and their "social" marginal product; the right-hand side has the opposite sign for a corresponding difference for the W's $(f' > 0)$. Hence if the M's get more than their marginal products when they invest in improving themselves, the W's must get less than theirs when they invest in themselves.

If the shares of M and W add to b rather than to one, equation (4.13) can be generalized to

$$(4.14) \qquad I_m^{*\,\prime} - bZ_m = f'(m)[bZ_w - I_w^{*\,\prime}],$$

where bZ_m is M's social marginal product, and similarly for W. Again, if the gain to M's from investment exceeds their social product, the gain to W's from investment must be less than their social product.

Moreover, such distorted incentives to invest become partly self-fulfilling. Since men would invest more, their high shares would appear to be justified by their productivity. Yet women would have invested more had they received their true marginal products in marriage markets.

As we have shown, if men and women marry for love, the equilibrium sortings are strongly positive, yet they would not be efficient if the cross derivative of the marital output function is negative. This is easily seen with the utility functions in equation (4.10), where the combined utility in each marriage is twice the marital output, and total utility in all marriages is twice the aggregate output. With a negative second derivative, aggregate output is maximized with a perfectly negative, not a positive, sorting. Equilibrium sortings are not efficient with negative cross derivatives of marital output because altruism and love prevent persons with high characteristics from agreeing to binding prenuptial agreements with potential mates with low characteristics.

6. Summary

Marriages are strongly segregated by race, religion, family background, education, IQ, age, and many other characteristics. If men and women maximize their marital incomes, and if the sharing of marital output between spouses is determined by the supply and demand for men and women with different characteristics, then marriage markets would induce strong segregation only if the characteristics of men and women are complements in the production of marital output. It does seem likely that most, but not all, characteristics are complements.

But the assumption that men and women simply maximize their marital incomes is not realistic since persons marrying in modern times have usually been in love. Even when characteristics are substitutes rather than complements, love induces positive sorting and possible substantial segregation among marriages.

That love increases rather than reduces marital segregation illustrates a more general principle: segregation tends to be weaker, not stronger, when marital sortings determine equilibrium prices. Effective suppression of prices by altruism or other factors raises the degree of segregation by reducing the ability of lower-quality persons to "bribe" higher-quality persons into becoming their mates.

That flexible prices reduce the degree of segregation is a general result that applies also to the sorting of persons into firms and other categories. Chapter 5 discusses these and other determinants of the sorting of persons into different neighborhoods.

Segregation and Integration in Neighborhoods

1. "Good" Neighbors

Marriage and the family have the most intimate and important social effects on behavior. Probably next in importance in influence are friends, colleagues, and fellow students and employees. But the primary determinants of these, especially for most young persons, are the neighborhoods where they grow up, attend school and church, and participate in sports and other group activities. To try to better understand these influences, this chapter considers how families choose neighborhoods that may differ in amenities, such as views, as well as in the composition of neighbors.

Following the assumption of Chapter 4 that participants in marriage markets generally agree ex ante on who are the most desirable mates, we assume that all families usually agree ex ante on who are the most desirable neighbors. Most of the time this is a realistic assumption, although Hispanics and Catholics, for example, may prefer living near other Hispanics or Catholics. The assumption that families agree on who is desirable is not only realistic but also makes the analytical problem of the allocation of heterogeneous families across neighborhoods far more interesting and challenging.

To simplify the analysis, most of the discussion (but see section 5) assumes only two neighborhoods, A and B. When there are only two neighborhoods, the gain from assuming many types of families is limited, so we assume only two types, H and L. Everyone agrees that the

H's are preferred as neighbors because the spillovers from them to their neighbors are more beneficial.

We assume that all families in the same neighborhood are equally "close." Some economists have introduced techniques from physics to provide more continuous definitions of neighbors (see Brock and Durlauf, 1995; Topa, 1996). These techniques are useful, but we will ignore them to put more emphasis on the distinctions caused by political jurisdictions as well as physical distance.

It is not reasonable when there are many "neighbors" to assume an aggregate output that is divided among neighbors by prices, or in other ways. Rather, it is more sensible to assume that families take the composition of their neighbors as given, and that their utility is directly affected by this composition. A natural and simple metric for composition is the proportion of all neighbors who are H's:

$$(5.1) \qquad s_j = \frac{H_j}{H_j + L_j}, \qquad \text{where } j = A \text{ or } B,$$

although the absolute number of neighbors (H + L) may also matter.

One major difference between marriage and neighborhoods is that whereas individuals (or their parents) can choose whom they marry, typically families cannot directly choose who will live near them. They do not usually own or control the other homes in their neighborhoods. This implies that even with flexible and competitive prices for housing, there may be important positive or negative spillovers when a family moves into a particular neighborhood. As a result of these spillovers, the allocation of families across neighborhoods may not be efficient in the sense of maximizing aggregate productivity or of being on the utility-possibility frontier.

There are many examples of spillovers among neighbors. Abler students tend to raise the learning of other students in the same school or neighborhood, drug addicts may steal from their neighbors and create an unpleasant living environment, welfare mothers in a neighborhood may validate collecting welfare and thereby induce other women in the neighborhood to have children out of wedlock. Better neighbors also increase the likelihood that one's children will make better marriages, since marriage is much more common between persons who live near each other. Neighbors may also improve networking and employment, since they often provide information about attractive job openings (see Topa, 1996). Some neighbors may provide prestige and even give a signal that a family is a better type than it really is.

For our purposes, whether productivity or utility is affected by neighbors is not important since in both cases a family's behavior is determined by its willingness to pay to have different types of neighbors. Obviously, a family's willingness to pay to live in a particular neighborhood depends on its own characteristics, including income, education, age, family composition, and preferences, and on the amenities of the neighborhood, including views of the sea and other scenery or proximity to good highways. However, willingness to pay may also depend in important ways on the characteristics of neighbors, as measured by s, the relative number of H's.

If we assume that all members of a given type, H or L, are identical, then the willingness to pay to live in a particular neighborhood for H's or L's depends on only two variables: the relative number of H's there, measured by s, and the amenities of the neighborhood, measured by Z:

(5.2)
$$V^j = V^j(s_i, Z_i), \quad \text{with} \quad \frac{\partial V^j}{\partial s} > 0, \frac{\partial V^j}{\partial Z_i} > 0$$

$$\text{for } j = H, L \quad \text{and} \quad i = A, B.$$

A family may be willing to pay more to live in a particular neighborhood because it has better amenities, better neighbors, or both. Moreover, the effects of one or both of these variables on the willingness-to-pay functions may differ between H and L families. Differences by type in these willingness-to-pay functions are the main determinant of the allocation of different types to different neighborhoods.

Throughout most of this chapter, we take the number and quality of houses in each neighborhood as given. However, section 6 does briefly discuss changes in zoning rules and other political restrictions on housing that affect the number and quality of houses allowed in a neighborhood. We assume for simplicity that the combined number of houses in both neighborhoods equals the total number of H's and L's, and that each family lives in one and only one house. Initially, we assume also that each neighborhood has an equal number of houses, N, although both assumptions are relaxed later in the chapter.

We have the following simple relation between the shares of H in neighborhoods A and B:

(5.3)
$$s_a + s_b = \frac{h}{N} = 2\left(\frac{h}{h+1}\right) = 2\bar{s},$$

where h and l are the number of H and L families, and $\bar{s}$ is the share of the H's in the total number of families.

2. Segregation and Integration with Competitive Prices

This section assumes a competitive market for housing in each neighborhood, so that a house is sold to the highest bidder, regardless of the wishes of neighbors. This means that the equilibrium prices of houses are the same to members of H and L, regardless of their characteristics. Which types live in which neighborhoods then is determined entirely by their willingness-to-pay functions.

We simplify these functions without much loss of interesting generality by assuming that the willingness to pay for amenities is separable from the willingness to pay for neighbor type. Then equation (5.2) can be written as

(5.4) $$V^j = u^j(Z_i) + f^j(s_i), \quad \text{with } u', f' > 0; u'' \le 0;$$
$$j = H, L \quad \text{and} \quad i = A, B.$$

Perhaps a more reasonable assumption is complementarity between social capital (measured by s) and own consumption (Z) so that $\partial^2 V/\partial Z \partial s > 0$. The marginal utility from consumption would then be bolstered by having more prestigious neighbors, perhaps because of the utility advantage from conspicuous consumption. As Chapter 8 shows, if these complementarities are sufficiently strong, the utility function might be convex in incomes after the effects of status and other income on social capital (measured in this chapter by s) are incorporated. This provides a stronger incentive to gamble and choose lotteries over income and status, although complementarity is not necessary to have lotteries (see Cole and Prescott, 1997, for a recent application of the demand for lotteries to the discussion of "clubs"). To simplify, until Chapter 8 we maintain the assumption of separability between consumption and s.

We start with the assumption that amenities are considered by both types to be the same in each neighborhood ($Z_a = Z_b = Z$), so that they do not affect the allocation of H's and L's between neighborhoods. Later, we will show that even small differences in amenities have interesting effects on prices and the degree of segregation and integration.

Given the assumption of equal amenities, competitive bidding, and that both H's and L's want to live near H's, it follows that equilibrium prices of houses are greater when the fraction of H's in a neighborhood is higher. The explanation is simply that everyone bids more to live near a larger number of H's. This has the interesting implication that neighborhoods would have different housing prices, even when they are *intrinsically identical*, simply because the composition of residents differs. Identical houses may sell for higher prices because they are in neighborhoods where other residents have higher incomes and other socially valued characteristics.

This effect of H's on housing prices helps define an equilibrium allocation of H's and L's between neighborhoods. An equilibrium has an allocation of H's and L's between neighborhoods, and sufficiently higher prices for houses in neighborhoods with larger fractions of H's, so that no one wants to change his neighborhood at these prices.

Such pricing equilibria could have varying degrees of integration and segregation between H's and L's. However, equal prices and full integration—the same proportion of H's in all neighborhoods—is always an equilibrium, because no single H or L then wants to change neighborhoods since physical and social amenities are the same in both. But full pooling or full integration may not be the only equilibrium, and these may not be stable.

A fully integrated pooling equilibrium has:

$$(5.5) \qquad P_a = P_b \quad \text{and} \quad s_a = s_b = \bar{s},$$

where P_i is the price of a house in the ith neighborhood.

There may also be partially segregated equilibria that would be symmetrical between A and B since they have the same amenities. For any equilibrium with less than full segregation, all H's and L's must be indifferent between the neighborhoods. This implies that

$$(5.6) \qquad f^h(s_a^*) - f^h(s_b^*) = f^l(s_a^*) - f^l(s_b^*) = P_a^* - P_b^*,$$

with

$$(5.7) \qquad P_a^* > P_b^* \quad \text{if} \quad s_a^* > s_b^*,$$

where $f^i(s_j)$, $i = H, L$, and $j = A, B$ are defined in equation (5.4) and measure willingness to pay to live near H's. If such an equilibrium exists, there is a symmetrical equilibrium with P_a, P_b, s_a^*, and s_b^* reversed.

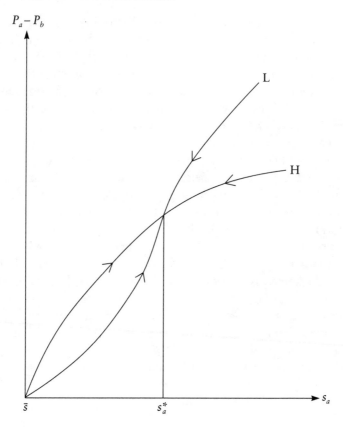

Figure 5.1

Equation (5.6) cannot be satisfied if the marginal willingness to pay to be in a neighborhood with more H's is always higher, or always lower, for H's than for L's, for then $f^h(s_a^*) - f^h(s_b^*) \neq f^l(s_a^*) - f^l(s_b^*)$. If H's marginal willingness to pay always exceeds L's (if $f'^h > f'^l$), the only equilibrium (other than full integration) must be fully segregated. Corresponding to equation (5.7) are the conditions $s_a^* = 1, s_b^* = 0$, and

(5.8) $$f^l(1) - f^l(0) < P_a - P_b < f^h(1) - f^h(0).$$

A symmetrical equilibrium has $s_a^* = 0, s_b^* = 1$. Since equation (5.6) only depends on the willingness-to-pay function at two points, a uniformly higher marginal willingness-to-pay function for H's is merely a sufficient condition for a fully segregated equilibrium. Any condition that makes H's more willing to pay than L's for all levels of $s > \bar{s}$ guarantees that full segregation is the only other equilibrium.

Figures 5.1 and 5.2 plot the willingness to pay of H and L to live in neighborhood A compared with B as determined by the relative number of H's in A. Equilibria occur where these functions intersect: twice in Figure 5.1 and once in 5.2. The price premium must be zero, $P_a - P_b = 0$, when $s_a^* = s_b^* = \bar{s}$ and so the L and H functions intersect at the origin in both figures. In Figure 5.1, they also intersect again when $\bar{s} < s_a^* < 1$. By symmetry, a corresponding equilibrium occurs when $\bar{s} < s_b^* < 1$.

In Figure 5.2, the functions only intersect at the fully integrated point, but there is a fully segregated equilibrium where $s_a^* = 1$. At that

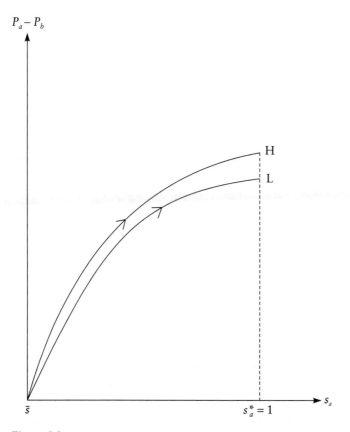

Figure 5.2

point, H's are willing to pay more to be with other H's than are L's. Again there is a corresponding fully segregated equilibrium, where s_a^* = 0 and $s_b^* = 1$.

Not all the equilibria in these figures are stable. A plausible concept of local stability of an equilibrium allocation of H's and L's between neighborhoods is that it depends on whether small deviations in the s's from an equilibrium set in motion pressure on prices and the allocation of H's and L's that force a return to the equilibrium. The fully integrated equilibria at $s_a^* = \bar{s}$ in Figures 5.1 and 5.2 are unstable because H's willingness-to-pay function is above L's to the right of these equilibria. Therefore a small increase in s_a from this point induces more H's than L's to try to get into this "better" category. They outbid the L's for houses, which makes s_a continue to rise until it reaches s_a^*; similarly at the symmetrical equilibrium for s_a^*.

This equilibrium at s_a^* in Figure 5.1 is stable because L's willingness-to-pay function is above H's beyond that point. Therefore small further increases in s_a induce L's to outbid the H's for these places, which forces s_a back to s_a^*. For the same reason, a fully segregated equilibrium, such as the one at $s_a^* = 1$ in Figure 5.2, is always locally stable. H's willingness-to-pay function must be above L's when s_a^* is near one since it is above L's when $s_a^* = 1$—that is precisely why full segregation is an equilibrium.

The local stability condition at an internal equilibrium, such as in Figure 5.1, requires that the L's want to be with additional H's more than the H's do. The full condition with only two neighborhoods is that the derivative of the equilibrium condition for L's in equation (5.6) exceeds the derivative of the same condition for H's. By differentiating and using the adding-up condition in equation (5.3), the stability condition when there is not full segregation translates into

(5.9)
$$f'^l(s_a^*) + f'^l(s_b^*) > f'^h(s_a^*) + f'^h(s_b^*).$$

The average slope of L's willingness to pay to be with H's at the two equilibrium levels of s must exceed the average slope of H's willingness to pay to be with other H's. This condition implies that if an H moves from B to A to replace an L who moves from A to B, thereby increasing s_a and reducing s_b, an L would then outbid an H for the "last" place in neighborhood A. This outbidding returns s_a to s_a^* and s_b to s_b^*.

A "partial" stability condition that is relevant if there are many small neighborhoods considers deviations only in s_a (or s_b) with no change in s_b (or s_a). The slope of L's willingness to pay to be with H's must then exceed that of H's at both equilibrium neighborhoods. In other words, stability then requires that small perturbations in the fraction of H's at either neighborhood alone affect L's more than H's. That is,

(5.10) $$f'^l(s_a^*) > f'^h(s_a^*) \quad \text{and} \quad f'^l(s_b^*) > f'^h(s_b^*).$$

Note that equation (5.10) is a stronger condition than (5.9), since (5.9) is satisfied if (5.10) is. See Appendix 7A for related stability conditions using the Cho and Kreps (1987) deviation criteria.

Neither stability condition is consistent with the equilibrium condition for both L's and H's in equation (5.6) if L's marginal willingness-to-pay function everywhere is above or below that of H's between s_b^* and s_a^*. For both the stability and equilibrium conditions to hold, in some interval or intervals between these two values of s, f'^l must be sufficiently below f'^h, and in other intervals it must be sufficiently above f'^h, so that the total difference between the f values of L and H, as in equation (5.6), is the same between s_a and s_b. This is a strong condition, so the presumption from this analysis is that many equilibria are likely to have either full segregation or full integration of homogeneous types.

3. Differences in Amenities

We have been assuming that both neighborhoods have the same amenities, and now we allow amenities to differ. Perhaps neighborhood A has more convenient access to shopping or freeways, or better views of a lake or river. We continue to assume, however, that each neighborhood has a fixed number of houses and an equal number of units, that each H and L buys only one house, and that the total number of houses equals the total number of H's and L's. We also assume, just to highlight the tendency toward segregation, that H and L have an equal number of members.

Assume that H's and L's value these amenities differently because the groups differ in wealth, education, and other characteristics that affect their willingness to pay for various kinds of amenities. To be concrete, let H's place a higher relative value on the amenities in A than L's do; it is even possible that H's prefer the amenities in A, while L's prefer those in B.

If both H's and L's only slightly prefer the amenities in one of these neighborhoods to those in the other, then the difference in amenities alone would not cause houses in A to sell for much more or less than those in B. For example, if H and L prefer the amenities in A to those in B only by 5 and 3 percent, respectively, the difference in amenities alone could not cause equilibrium prices of A houses to be more than 5 percent higher than B houses.

Indeed, if people do not care about their "neighbors"—that is, they do not care who owns the other houses in the same neighborhood—all H's would buy in A, all L's would buy in B, and houses in A would sell for a premium that would be too steep for L's but would be acceptable to H's. This implies that A's would then sell for between 3 and 5 percent more than B's.

But even mild concern at the margin about neighbors can have a large effect on the equilibrium difference in prices of houses in A and B, and possibly even change radically who lives in A and B. Suppose that H's and L's care equally about being neighbors of H's, so that their willingness to pay to live in A or B increases at the same rate as the share of H's in A or B increases.

Therefore, consider again the separable willingness-to-pay function in equation (5.4), and assume that the $f(s)$ functions are the same for H's and L's:

$$(5.11) \qquad V_i^j = u^j(Z_i) + f(s_i), \qquad j = H, L \quad \text{and} \quad i = A, B.$$

Let

$$(5.12) \qquad u^h(Z_a) - u^h(Z_b) = \varepsilon^h > \varepsilon^l = u^l(Z_a) - u^l(Z_b),$$

where $\varepsilon^h > \varepsilon^l$ is small, and ε^l could even be negative. There is competitive bidding for houses in A and B, which determine equilibrium prices, P_a and P_b, and equilibrium shares of H's: s_a^* and s_b^*.

If segregation were incomplete, the analogue of equation (5.6) would have to hold. This equation implies

$$(5.13) \qquad P_a - P_b = u^h(Z_a^*) - u^h(Z_b^*) + f(s_a^*) - f(s_b^*)$$

$$= u^l(Z_a^*) - u^l(Z_b^*) + f(s_a^*) - f(s_b^*)$$

$$= \varepsilon^h + f(s_a^*) - f(s_b^*) = \varepsilon^l + f(s_a^*) - f(s_b^*).$$

However, equations (5.11) and (5.12) imply that this condition cannot hold since $\varepsilon^h > \varepsilon^l$. Therefore the only equilibrium must have complete segregation, where all H's live in A, and all L's live in B. There is no fully integrating equilibrium, nor a symmetrical segregating equilibrium, where all the H's live in B and all the L's live in A.

Equation (5.8) implies that at the unique and fully segregating equilibrium, the difference between the prices of housing in A and B is bounded by

$$(5.14) \qquad \varepsilon^l + f(1) - f(0) < P_a - P_b < \varepsilon^h + f(1) - f(0).$$

One might expect that since both ε^h and ε^l are small because the amenities in A are valued only a little differently than those in B, housing in A would sell for only a little more than housing in B. But equation (5.14) shows that this expectation is false if radical differences in the proportion of H's in a neighborhood has sizable effects on willingness to pay.

If $f(1) - f(0)$ is large, houses in A carry a large premium even if both H and L only slightly prefer the amenities in A compared with B. Moreover, the marginal effect of an increase in the population of H's in a neighborhood, given by the derivative $\partial f/\partial s$, need not be large for the equilibrium difference in prices to be huge. For the price difference is caused not by the *slope* of the willingness-to-pay function for desirable neighbors, but by the *integral* over the entire interval of possible values of the population of desirable neighbors.

The interesting dynamics of this process is shown in Figure 5.3, which plots the willingness to pay of H and L for a house in A compared to B as a function of s_a (in this case, $s_b = 1 - s_a$). At full integration where $s_a = s_b = \frac{1}{2}$, H's are willing to pay slightly more than L's for houses in A. As additional H's bid for houses in A, s_a and P_a rise, and the increase in s_a raises the desires of both H's and L's to live in A. But since these desires increase at the same rate, H's still want to live there

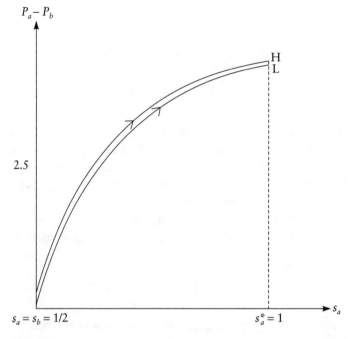

Figure 5.3

more than L's do even at the higher value of s_a, and more expensive housing in A. Prices in A and the number of H's in A rise still further, but this too fails to narrow the gap between the willingness to pay of H's and L's to live in A. The process is repeated until all H's live in A, and the price of houses there greatly exceeds the price of similar housing in B.

Therefore, when willingness to pay for "good" neighbors is the same for H's and L's, the choice of neighborhoods by H and L is fully determined by their valuation of amenities. In this case, all H's buy A's and all L's buy B's because H values the amenities in A more than L does. However, the competition to have H's as neighbors forces the price of housing in A much above the amenity value of A. The price of living in A depends on how much the willingness-to-pay functions of H's and L's rise as more and more neighbors in A become H's.

What appears to be strange about this result is that H's would have to pay an enormous premium to live in A even though they only slightly prefer A to B—in Figure 5.3, $P_a^* - P_b^* > 2.5 >> \varepsilon_h$. But they are willing to pay such a premium for A *only* because other H's also live in A. Although it might *appear* that they are paying the premium for the quality of the scenery or other amenities offered by A, in fact H's are paying the premium mainly to be neighbors of one another. It is the competition from L's to live in A, where they have more H's as neighbors, which forces the premium on A's amenities to such a high level.

Veblen, in his *Theory of the Leisure Class,* reaches a similar conclusion when he recognizes that beautiful objects may sell for many times the utility derived from their beauty because of the honor conferred by their possession: "It frequently happens that an article which serves the honorific purpose of conspicuous waste is at the same time a beautiful object . . . But the utility . . . is commonly due less to their intrinsic beauty than to the honor which their possession and consumption confers" (1934, pp. 128–129).

Although full integration is never an equilibrium if H's and L's value the amenities of A and B differently, a unique partial integration may be an equilibrium if L's marginal willingness to pay to be with H's exceeds H's willingness to pay. Figure 5.4 provides an example of a stable equi-

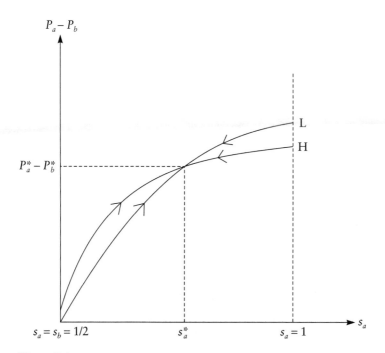

Figure 5.4

librium with partial segregation of H's and L's, where $s_a^* > s_b^*$. It is not surprising that differences between H's and L's in their evaluation of A's amenities should increase the degree of segregation. Highly integrated equilibria become less likely since H's prefer to live in A more than L's do when neighbors in B are about as likely to be H's as are neighbors in A.

It is even possible to have a stable competitive equilibrium where houses in B are much more expensive than houses in A, even though *everyone* prefers the amenities of A to those of B (see $P_a^* - P_b^* < 0$ in Figure 5.5). At this equilibrium, houses in B are more expensive than in A because more H's live in B than in A ($s_a^* < \frac{1}{2}$). This is why both H's and L's may prefer B to A even when A is cheaper, and both types prefer A's amenities. They are willing to pay much more to live in B only because both H's and L's very much want H's as neighbors.

The paradox about this locally stable equilibrium in Figure 5.5 is

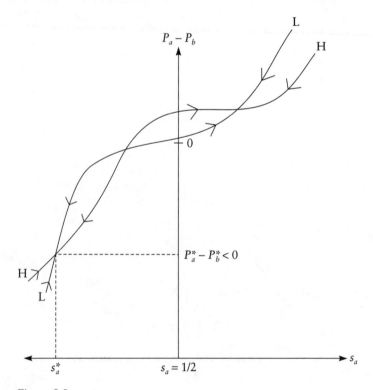

Figure 5.5

that most H's live in the neighborhood with the worse amenities, even though they are willing to pay more for better amenities than L's are. Yet individual H's who pay a much higher price to live in B do not sell their houses and move to A, even though they prefer A's amenities, because neighbors in B are much more likely to be other H's. Of course, H's who live in B would gain from collectively selling their houses there and buying cheaper houses in A, but we assume these are decentralized markets where everyone acts independently.

4. Competition and Efficiency

When people bid for places in large categories, like neighborhoods, they generally do not take account of the positive or negative effects of their entry on other members, except insofar as that affects how neighbors treat them. But since everyone is assumed to want to be with the H's, entry of L's lowers the utilities of *all* neighbors, L's as well as H's. Similarly, entry of H's raises the utility of *all* neighbors. In other words, H's and L's in a neighborhood impose positive and negative spillovers on all other residents of the same neighborhood, spillovers that generally are not internalized with private competitive bidding for houses.

These spillovers would be internalized if both H and L residents of a neighborhood could get together and make joint offers to potential residents. They would offer lower housing prices to H's, since having more H's would raise their own utilities. The housing "discount" they would be willing to offer H's depends on the effect of H's on their own utilities, measured by their aggregate willingness to pay.

Such collective bidding by members of each neighborhood is one way to obtain an efficient allocation of members among neighborhoods. For each family would be allocated to that neighborhood where the other residents are willing to pay the most to have it as a neighbor. Since we assume there are no spillovers *between* neighborhoods, such bidding would maximize the aggregate willingness to pay over all neighborhoods and families.

But with large neighborhoods, such as those in a reasonably sized town or city district, residents generally do not collectively bid for other residents—except through laws and regulations as discussed in section 6. Instead, they compete for houses, taking account of the composition of the residents in a neighborhood. With individual bidding, the allocation of types among neighborhoods is generally not efficient because the competitive equilibrium allocation of families depends on individual willingness to pay, not on the aggregate willingness that incorporates spillovers among neighborhoods.

Competitive allocations are defined by equations (5.6)–(5.8), which depend on the amounts each family is willing to pay to be in one neighborhood rather than the other. By contrast, efficiency incorporates all these spillovers, and depends on the effect of each family on the *aggregate* willingness to pay of all neighbors.

While it is rather obvious that competitive allocations generally are not efficient when everyone wants to be with the preferred type, it is less clear a priori whether competitive allocations are biased toward too much or too little segregation of types. However, with concave willingness-to-pay functions, competitive bidding generally results in too much neighborhood segregation between the more and the less preferred types.

In our formulation, the willingness to pay by each H and L depends on s, the fraction of their neighbors who are H's. The aggregate willingness to pay by the H and L residents of neighborhood i is given by

$$(5.15) \qquad W_i = N[s_i f^h(s_i) + (1 - s_i)f^l(s_i)], \qquad i = A, B.$$

This aggregate willingness to pay by residents depends on the fraction of H's who live there and also on neighborhood amenities, but the amenities effect is unimportant since in this section both neighborhoods are assumed to have the same amenities.

If we suppress the constant N, the total willingness to pay over both neighborhoods, W, is then

$$(5.16) \qquad W = W_a + W_b = s_a f^h(s_a) + s_b f^h(s_b) + (1 - s_a)f^l(s_a) + (1 - s_b)f^l(s_b)$$

An efficient allocation chooses s_a and s_b to maximize W, subject to the adding-up constraint in equation (5.3).

Let the aggregate willingness to pay of H be

$$(5.17) \qquad IV^h = N[s_a f^h(s_a) + s_b f^h(s_b)],$$

and similarly for L. If total willingness to pay of each group is a concave function, then the total willingness to pay is maximized with full integration ($s_a = s_b$). If both f functions are convex, full segregation maximizes $N_h V^h$ and $N_l V^l$. If the aggregate willingness-to-pay functions are concave in some regions and convex in others, the efficient allocation may have partial segregation.

However, a competitive market for housing does not necessarily lead to full integration even when both willingness-to-pay functions are concave. We can show the difference between the efficient and competitive outcomes by differentiating the aggregate willingness to pay, W, with respect to s_a—taking account of the adding-up condition. If the optimal is not at a corner $(0 < s_a < 2\bar{s})$, then this first-order condition (FOC) for efficiency is

(5.18)
$$[(f_a^h - f_b^h) - (f_a^l - f_b^l)] + [s_a f_a'^h - s_b f_b'^h]$$

$$+ [(1 - s_a)f_a'^l - (1 - s_b)f_b'^l] = 0,$$

where $f'(s_j)$ is the change in f as s_j changes.

Contrasting equation (5.6) with equation (5.18) shows why the degree of segregation produced by competitive allocations may differ from the segregation that maximizes aggregate willingness to pay. Competition equalizes the differences in the willingness to pay of H's and L's to be with H's. Although the efficient degree of segregation also depends on this difference—the first bracketed term in equation (5.18)—in addition it depends on the concavity or convexity in the willingness-to-pay functions of each group—the second and third bracketed terms. Put differently, at a competitive equilibrium, the first bracketed term of equation (5.18) is zero, but the sum of the other two bracketed terms need not be zero. These terms depend on the slopes at the competitive equilibrium of the willingness-to-pay functions of H and L in the different neighborhoods, and on the relative number of H's and L's in each neighborhood at that equilibrium.

Although the relation in (5.18) looks complicated, it yields a simple and important result about whether competition leads to too much or too little neighborhood segregation. Essentially, the competitive equilibrium ignores the degree of concavity or convexity in the individual willingness-to-pay functions. By ignoring this, the competitive equilibrium tends to encourage excessive segregation if these functions are concave functions of the number of "elites" in a neighborhood. For then $f_a'^h < f_b'^h$, and $f_a'^l < f_b'^l$ at the competitive equilibrium if $s_a > s_b$, and the derivative of the total willingness to pay with respect to s_a (the left-hand side of equation 5.18) would be negative at the competitive equilibrium.

We have derived a fundamental proposition (Proposition 5.1): If the willingness-to-pay functions of H and L are everywhere concave, the efficient degree of segregation that maximizes aggregate willingness to pay is generally less than the degree of segregation at any stable competitive equilibrium. To prove Proposition 5.1 formally, rewrite equation (5.18) at the competitive equilibrium with $s_a^* > s_b^*$ as

$$(5.19) \qquad \partial W/\partial s_a^* = [(f_a^h - f_b^h) - (f_a^l - f_b^l)] + s_a^*(f_a'^h - f_b'^h)$$

$$+ (1 - s_a^*)(f_a'^l - f_b'^l) + (s_a^* - s_b^*)(f_b'^h - f_b'^l)$$

The bracketed term is zero by the competitive condition in equation (5.6). The next two terms are both negative by the assumptions that f is concave and $s_a^* > s_b^*$. The last term is negative by the stability condition for a competitive equilibrium. Hence, $\partial W/\partial s_a^* < 0$, so that there is socially "excessive" segregation at the competitive position $s_a^* > s_b^*$. De Bartolome (1990) gives the first published proof of a very closely related proposition; other applications include Benabou (1993); we (Becker and Murphy, 1994) derived this proposition at about the same time.

Note that the converse of Proposition 5.1 does not necessarily follow: a competitive equilibrium may not have too little segregation if the willingness-to-pay functions are convex. This is clear from equation (5.19); the bracketed term is still zero and the last term is still negative by the stability condition, but the two middle terms are positive by convexity. However, if the willingness-to-pay functions are very convex, the competitive equilibrium will then tend to have less segregation than is socially optimal.

This proposition may not hold if there is heterogeneity within H's and L's, so that members of each group differ in their willingness to be with H's. But if the H's differ, the amount a family is willing to pay to have good neighbors may not depend only on the relative number of H's, but also on which of the H's are its neighbors. In that case, we effectively have many rather than two groups. Hence the qualification of the proposition due to within-group heterogeneity is really a call to analyze more than two groups.

One might have expected competitive bidding for houses to produce too little, rather than too much, segregation of the "desirable" types relative to the efficient degree of segregation. For a competitive market is not able to charge L's higher prices in order to deter them from entering more segregated neighborhoods where they lower utilities of the mainly H occupants. However, it is equally true that competitive markets do not charge lower prices to H's to induce them to enter more integrated neighborhoods where they raise everyone's utility. Our proposition shows that the latter force is more important when willingness-to-pay functions of H and L are concave.

The degree of neighborhood segregation by race, income, age, marital status, families with or without small children, and other characteristics is often considered excessive when judged by the welfare of the groups who are less represented in more desirable neighborhoods. The degree of segregation is usually attributed in part to discrimination against "undesirable" groups by residents of neighborhoods they want to enter, sometimes through political manipulation of zoning and other public policies that discriminate against these groups (see section 6). For example, the famous *Brown* Supreme Court decision attacked southern racial school segregation because of the belief that it hurt black students (see Brown v. Board of Education, 1954). However, Proposition 5.1 implies that the degree of segregation under free competition for housing could be attacked without emphasizing the effect only on minorities, because everyone could be made better off with less segregation.

The implication of blaming political discrimination for neighborhood segregation is that free competition without political discrimination would produce close to the socially "optimal" degree of segregation. Proposition 5.1 shows that this implication is false—and for certain, if bidding functions are concave. Even without any discrimination in prices or public policies, free competition for housing then produces excessive, possibly greatly excessive, segregation compared with the allocation that maximizes aggregate willingness to pay. Therefore, uniform prices to everyone bidding for the same neighborhood do not provide enough prices or markets to internalize all the spillovers between types.

The implication of this proposition about excess segregation under competition applies not only to residential neighborhoods, but also to other kinds of categories where most people prefer to be with the "desirable" types, such as owners of fashionable clothing or collectors of classic cars. Proposition 5.1 states that competitive bidding for these objects also leads to excess segregation of the more desirable types (see Chapters 6 and 7).

This proposition does not apply when there is effectively a single owner of all places in a category. A company, for example, takes account of the tastes and productivities of its employees in determining wages to employees. It would be willing to pay higher wages to employees who have positive effects on productivities or utilities of other employees.

The allocation of employees that results from such behavior has produced considerable segregation among firms of women and other minorities (see, for example, Carrington and Troske, 1998a, b). However, since firms internalize all spillovers among their employees, the degree of market segregation in this case would not be "excessive" in the limited sense that nondiscriminating competitive firms maximize aggregate willingness to pay over *all* their employees.

5. Competition and Free Entry among Neighborhoods

The analysis so far in this chapter is based on the assumption of two neighborhoods of given size, where "neighborhood" is defined by political jurisdiction or as land owned by a "developer." For some purposes, however, a more relevant model has many small neighborhoods engaged in competition for residents, similar to a Tiebout model of competition among local governments. Moreover, the size of neighborhoods may change due to construction of new housing and deterioration of old housing, the joining together of separate jurisdictions, or the splitting of a given jurisdiction into two or more independent political entities.

If many small neighborhoods compete for residents—perhaps each one is controlled by a developer—full segregation would then be a feasible equilibrium because it could always satisfy an adding-up condition such as in equation (5.3): some neighborhoods may have only H's, others would have only L's, and the fraction with only H's guarantees that the adding-up condition is satisfied. By contrast, complete segregation is possible with two neighborhoods only in the "accidental" case where the number of L's and H's and the size of each neighborhood is just right to satisfy the adding-up condition.

If all land is homogeneous but if the amount of land exceeds the demand for space, some "neighborhoods" may have no residents. Other neighborhoods may only have poor residents, or ethnic and racial minorities. Land would be free in these neighborhoods because residents in segregated neighborhoods only pay for the land, and competition from unused land would force basic land prices to zero.

If land were also free in neighborhoods with H's, that would attract L's from the segregated L neighborhoods, unless the developers of these H neighborhoods directly discriminated against L's, possibly by charging L's higher prices for space. However, discrimination may not be legal; moreover, higher prices to L's, even if legal, may be impossible to maintain as housing gets resold.

Therefore we continue to assume, as in previous sections, that L and H residents of the same neighborhood pay the same price for land. Then the only way neighborhoods with some H's can limit the number of L's is by "discriminating" indirectly. Developers can bid up the competitive cost of land to everyone in their neighborhoods by improving the quality of living through various acreage restrictions and other amenities that raise utility, and also land prices, to all residents. The cost of providing these amenities must be high enough to eliminate any profits to developers; otherwise, residents of integrated neighborhoods would be bid away by developers with empty land.

This section only illustrates some of the complications and different results that arise when there is competition among many neighborhoods. Many of the analytical issues that arise are similar to those discussed in the extensive literature on signaling equilibria. Appendix 7A uses some of this literature to discuss the stability of segregated and pooling equilibria.

Consider the case where in equilibrium, some L's are in fully segregated neighborhoods with free land. If other L's are in partially integrated neighborhoods, then all L's must be indifferent between all neighborhoods, given the cost of land and the quality of amenities in the integrated neighborhoods. Figure 5.6 explores the equilibrium in this case by plotting the indifference curves of L and H between the cost of land and the share of H's (s) in a particular neighborhood. These indifference curves are obviously positively sloped, and we assume they are also concave because the willingness to pay for more H's is concave. The equilibrium indifference curve for L is labeled L^*. It goes through the origin because L's in neighborhoods with $s > 0$ receive the same utility as those in neighborhoods with only L's and free land.

To examine first whether complete segregation of both L's and H's is an equilibrium, let H' be the indifference curve of H that goes through L^* when $s = 1$. In Figure 5.6, H' is assumed to lie above L^* to the left

Cost of land

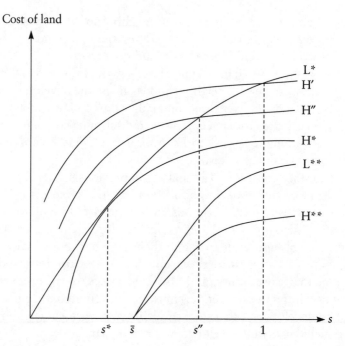

Figure 5.6

of $s = 1$, so that complete segregation—neighborhoods with $s = 1$ and $s = 0$—would seem to be a stable equilibrium. For if $s < 1$, H's are willing to pay more than L's to get into these partially integrated neighborhoods. Recall that the stability condition in the two neighborhood case is that the willingness-to-pay function of L's cuts that of H's from below, as in Figures 5.2 and 5.3, and also in Figure 5.6.

But that is not enough to guarantee a stable equilibrium when many neighborhoods compete for residents. Consider a developer of another neighborhood who offers slightly less than complete segregation, say $s = s''$ in Figure 5.6. For L's to be indifferent between partial integration and complete segregation, the relevant indifference curve of H (H'') must lie on L* at $s = s''$. Since H' cuts L* from above, H'' must also cut L* from above if s'' is close to 1.

Since H'' lies below H', H's are better off on L* with $s = s''$ than with $s = 1$. H's are better off with less than complete segregation because they are not willing to pay as much as L's for an increase in s from s'' to 1—that is the meaning of H' being flatter than L* at $s = 1$. Therefore, developers could attract H's more easily to neighborhoods with $s = s''$ < 1 than with $s = 1$, while L's would be indifferent to these neighborhoods, as long as the cost of land and amenities makes L's utility lie along L^*.

Although it appears in this case as if complete segregation is a locally stable equilibrium, complete segregation of both H's and L's could not survive the competition from neighborhoods with partial pooling of H's and L's (s either $=0$ or <1). The reason is that H's strictly prefer a mixed neighborhood to all H neighborhoods because the cost of keeping out *all* L's by raising amenities and the cost of land sufficiently is not worth enough to H's.

However, if H'' cuts L^* from above, s'' also would not be an equilibrium because an indifference curve of H ($\tilde{H}$) at an $\tilde{s} < s''$ that goes through L^* would also be above L^* (but below H''). This argument implies that the degree of segregation of H's continues to fall until it reaches an s^* where the indifference curve of H, H^*, is tangent to L^* (see Figure 5.6 at $s = s^*$).

Tangency implies that H^* lies below L^* both to the right and to the left of $s = s^*$. The utility of H's is maximized at s^*, given that L's are as well off as they are in fully segregated neighborhoods with free land. For H^* is the maximal utility of H's, given that L is on L^*—the minimal feasible utility for L's—and given also that competition with zero profits to developers determines land prices and amenities.

However, this efficient equilibrium on L^* at $s = s^*$ has only one-sided stability. The equilibrium is stable for $s > s^*$ since L^* is steeper than and above H^* to the right of s^*. However, it is not stable for $s < s^*$ since L^* is flatter than and above H^* also to the left of s^*. That is, neighborhoods with $s = s^*$ are partially unstable, and could "tip" into becoming fully segregated L neighborhoods.

Of course, if a particular mixed neighborhood tips toward becoming an all-L neighborhood, the H's who formerly resided in this neighborhood would move to other partially integrated neighborhoods. That is, the *overall* distribution of neighborhoods between those with $s = 0$ and those with $s = s^*$ would be stable, but not the composition of any particular integrated neighborhood.

Tipping of neighborhoods at unstable equilibria was early emphasized by Schelling (1978). Our analysis shows that tipping equilibria do not require collusion on the part of real estate brokers, or deterioration in the quality of housing. Tipping is "implied" by competition among neighborhoods even when property is not deteriorating, as long as enough neighborhoods compete, and some neighborhoods are fully segregated with "minorities." This tipping competitive equilibrium has analytical similarities to the "fad" monopoly equilibria considered in Chapter 9, since both have one-way instability.

However, the equilibrium at s^* is only efficient given free entry of L's and H's into neighborhoods, and no rationing or price discrimination. For this equilibrium has "rent dissipation." Competition increases amenities and the cost of land in neighborhoods with $s = s^*$ until L's are indifferent between s^* and $s = 0$. If developers or governments could ration entry of L's into neighborhoods with $s = s^*$, it would not be necessary to raise amenities and land prices in order to prevent L's from entering these neighborhoods.

The equilibrium at s^* clearly favors the H's since their utility is maximized, given that L's receive the minimal feasible utility for them. Developers pay greater attention to the desires of the H's because both L's and H's are willing to pay more to live in neighborhoods with relatively many H's. Hence developers can get higher prices for their land if they can find ways to attract H's (see also the discussion in Chapter 7).

Obviously, a distribution of neighborhoods with either $s = 0$ or $s = s^*$ is feasible only if the overall relative number of H's, $\bar{s}$, is less than s^*. Moreover, if $\bar{s} > s^*$, an equilibrium with $s = 0$ and $s = s' > \bar{s} > s^*$ is not feasible, for we have seen that $s' > s^*$ cannot survive competition from other neighborhoods with $s < s'$. Given $\bar{s} > s^*$, and the shape of the indifference curves assumed in Figure 5.6, the only equilibrium appears to be one with complete integration or pooling, where $s = \bar{s} > s^*$ in all neighborhoods. Competition from empty neighborhoods would drive the cost of land to zero in all neighborhoods.

This equilibrium is shown in Figure 5.6 at the point on the horizontal axis (where land is free) at $s = \bar{s}$. For this equilibrium to be stable, the indifference curve of L must be steeper than that of H, as in this figure. There is no rent dissipation and no segregation at this equilibrium.

Even if $\bar{s} < s^*$, the aggregate equilibrium with $s = s^*$ and $s = 0$ may not survive defection to full integration. It is also necessary that full integration (all $s = \bar{s}$) and free land put H on a lower utility level than H^*. Otherwise, both H's and L's would defect to such neighborhoods with full integration.

Depending on the shape of the indifference curves of H's and L's, there may be equilibria where some neighborhoods are fully segregated with H's and some are partially integrated, and there are still other possible outcomes. In all cases, however, developers want to make neighborhoods attractive to H's since that raises the willingness to pay to be in these neighborhoods of *both* L's and H's.

6. Segregation by Governments

Our analysis implies that competitive housing markets tend to produce excessive segregation between neighborhoods among different races, religions, income levels, and so on relative to the efficient level of segregation that maximizes the aggregate willingness to pay of all families. Yet during much of the past millennium, governments in most of the world encouraged segregation rather than desegregation.

For example, European governments forced Jews to live in separate neighborhoods—which gave rise to the term "ghetto." The Chinese empire for centuries required Arab and European traders to live in segregated neighborhoods of its cities. Until 1948, the federal government of the United States enforced restrictive covenants on housing deeds that prevented houses from being sold to blacks, Jews, and other minorities.

The discrimination against blacks by governments and the private sector in the United States housing market can be documented with evidence on housing prices. Our analysis implies that in freely competitive housing markets where most whites and many blacks prefer to have whites as neighbors, whites would have to pay a housing premium for the "privilege" of having mainly white neighbors.

Yet housing prices in 1950 suggest just the opposite, that blacks rather than whites paid relatively more for their housing when the degree of segregation was greater. See the excellent paper by Cutler, Glaeser, and Vidgor, 1999. They attribute this apparent paradox both to government enforcement of restricted covenants in housing deeds against blacks, and to direct government discrimination against blacks in the housing market (see also the analysis by Becker, 1957 [1971]).

Starting in the late 1950s, the federal government began to outlaw discrimination against blacks and other minorities in public schools, employment, and housing. And Cutler, Glaeser, and Vidgor do find a significant reversal in 1990 of their results for 1950. As the degree of segregation increased in a city in 1990, whites rather than blacks had to pay relatively more for "comparable" housing.

While outright government and other discrimination is no longer legal, subtler forms of government and private discrimination against blacks and other minorities are still possible. This discrimination relies on the result from section 3 that the degree of segregation under competition is greater when different groups value neighborhood amenities differently.

Therefore, suburban and other communities that want to discourage blacks, the poor, and other "undesirable" groups from bidding for houses in their communities may produce "amenities" that appeal less to these groups than to the rich, whites, Catholics, or other groups they want to attract. This hidden form of government discrimination may help explain highly restrictive zoning requirements, housing codes that add greatly to the cost of building houses, and generous spending on schools, swimming pools, and other public activities that raise property taxes.

Such requirements may discourage "undesirables" from living in a community even though a local government actively enforces laws against discrimination in its housing market. Such hidden discrimination is hard to detect, and it is often a more "wasteful" way to segregate the housing market than outright discrimination. But the laws against explicit discrimination may encourage majorities to find ways to discriminate in more subtle ways.

The basic proposition of this chapter proves a tendency toward excessive segregation in competitive housing markets compared with the "efficient" degree of segregation that maximizes aggregate willingness to pay. Departures from efficiency increase when governments discriminate among groups in hidden ways, for government discrimination through choice of "amenities" tends to be determined by the influence of the more powerful interest groups in their community, such as rich white families. Since even free competition without discrimination in housing markets leads to excessive segregation, government discrimination would further increase the degree of segregation and reduce efficiency.

Governments may also use their political power to narrow or widen the political boundaries of their communities. Restricting the boundaries of a suburb or other community may not change the physical proximity of residents of adjoining communities, but it does enormously affect their access to public schools and other public facilities provided by a community.

For example, white flight to the suburbs to avoid having their children go to public schools with many black children and other minorities is made easier by the small size of most suburban communities. Black and Hispanic children in Chicago, or in more open suburbs like

Evanston or Oak Park, cannot attend the same schools and other public facilities available to the mainly white children in Glencoe and other North Shore suburban communities.

Therefore, subtle discrimination through restricting the size of a community also adds to the degree of segregation in schools and other public facilities by limiting access to these facilities. Even when sizable scale public economies would be achieved through consolidation of adjacent communities, consolidation may be resisted because it integrates the use of these facilities.

At the turn of this century, Brooklyn voluntarily merged with New York City and Hyde Park voted to join the city of Chicago. We doubt they would agree to these mergers if the opportunity arose now rather than a century ago—few suburbs in recent years have voted to become part of their neighboring cities—partly because that would require much greater integration of their school systems. Indeed, the pressure is toward secession rather than integration, as mainly white Staten Island residents periodically clamor for independence from the rest of New York City, northern Californians occasionally agitate for separation from mostly Hispanic southern California, and many French-speaking residents of Quebec want to separate from the English-speaking part of Canada.

CHAPTER 6

The Social Market for the Great Masters and Other Collectibles

(with William Landes)

1. Motivation: Social Action at a Distance

The influence of the attitudes and behavior of others on a person's behavior is obvious within families, and is also rather apparent among neighbors, students in the same primary and secondary schools, and employees in the same companies. In all these cases, there is considerable direct interaction among members of the same category, be it the same neighborhood, family, school, or company.

But social pressures also sometimes have a powerful influence at a distance, even without physical contacts between those affected. For example, demand is often stimulated for goods that are more popular, including popular restaurants, books, concerts, colorful nail polish, clothing styles, decorating schemes, art and architecture, professional sports teams, and political candidates. There is seldom much, if any, direct contact between persons who own the same type of goods, yet what others consume often greatly affects what a person wants to buy.

Chapters 1 and 2 discuss several factors that contribute to the powerful influence of popularity. In many cases, popularity may raise demand because individuals who go to unpopular restaurants or engage in unpopular activities lose prestige and social standing.

Frequently, however, demand is influenced not by what is generally popular but, rather, by what is popular with more prestigious participants. Chapter 3 gives several reasons why such "leaders" influence the desires of more numerous "followers." Leaders may have greater knowledge of art or of other objects and goods; followers may gain acceptance and prestige by emulating the behavior of leaders; or followers may "pass" for leaders if they duplicate the behavior of leaders. This last motive is an example of Veblen's (1934) emphasis on conspicuous consumption to display wealth, possibly to create a false impression of being wealthy.

Many high school students try to emulate the behavior not of the majority of other students, but of star athletes and "cool" students (see Coleman, 1961). The length of skirts and styles of other clothing worn by women are usually determined by what is worn by fashion "leaders" in their circle of friends, or by designers and fashion trendsetters. Collectors of art and antiques may want to acquire the type of objects that are owned by prestigious collectors or recommended by experts and others considered to have greater knowledge.

2. Conditions of Supply

Our analysis of the allocation of families among neighborhoods in Chapter 5 generally assumes that the number of houses in each neighborhood is fixed. This is an excellent assumption for the short run, but housing supply in a neighborhood may eventually change greatly as new housing is built, high rises may replace single-family homes, and older housing may depreciate and decline in importance over time.

Indeed for most goods and activities, new supply can greatly affect the available quantity. With competition and free entry of producers, in the long run all units of the same good must sell at the cost of producing new units. This ability to produce additional units has enormous implications for the equilibrium derived in Chapter 5 regarding housing prices in different neighborhoods, as considered in section 5 of that chapter.

In equilibria with fixed supply, housing with "better" neighbors sells for more than equivalent housing in other neighborhoods. But if supply is augmentable, identical units must sell for the same price, even though consumers may be willing to pay much more to consume the same class of goods that the rich and other "leaders" consume.

Chapter 7 analyzes these and other major implications of production for the ability of markets to separate consumptions of leaders and followers. That chapter considers markets with free entry of competitive producers, and also markets where producers have monopoly power due to trademarks, copyrights, and other reasons.

This chapter, however, follows the discussion of neighborhoods in Chapter 5 by assuming a fixed number of identical units in each category of collectibles. Indeed, the assumption of a given fixed supply is especially appropriate for art and other antiquities, such as paintings, sculpture, and pottery by great masters of the past, antique furniture and hand-woven rugs, old photos, calligraphy, prints, first editions of books, and rare coins and stamps.

Moreover, the assumption of a more or less fixed supply applies not only to objects produced centuries ago but also to certain recently produced objects, such as paintings by Jackson Pollock and other celebrated deceased modern artists, objects that were formerly owned by Jacqueline Kennedy or Princess Diana, and rookie baseball cards of players who became superstars, such as Mickey Mantle or Willie Mays.

Although the supply of antiques is sometimes increased by discoveries of neglected work, a more serious issue is raised by copies and forgeries that escape detection. Section 4 considers the effects of copies and forgeries on prices of antiquities and other collectibles.

For all the reasons stated in section 1, the demand for many classes of collectible objects is enhanced when consumers of these objects are rich, renowned for their achievements as entertainers, politicians, or businessmen, and sometimes even when they are notorious scoundrels. This is why prominent individuals often hide their interest in objects to be auctioned by having intermediaries bid for them. They know that demand for, and hence the price to them, of these objects would increase if their interest became common knowledge.

Similarly, sellers of objects highlight previous owners who were prominent: a good history and pedigree can significantly raise market value (see Landes and Posner, 1996). Indeed, the objects owned by Jacqueline Kennedy auctioned a few years ago were undistinguished, and they fetched remarkably high prices only because she had owned them.

The impossibility of adding to supply—aside from forgeries—makes antiquities and modern collectibles particularly effective markets to separate out types of buyers. For as we have seen, this separation is impossible if new units are freely producible at a more or less constant cost. Consequently, not only does empirical evidence indicate that prestige and other characteristics of consumers sometimes greatly affect the pricing of antiquities, but our analysis explains why the separation of consumer by type is especially important in markets for many kinds of collectibles.

3. Pricing of Great Masters and Other Collectibles

The main issue considered in this section is the "superstar" phenomenon among old masters, antiquities, and other collectibles. For example, Rembrandt is considered a better artist than other even quite good Flemish painters of the sixteenth century, but does quality alone explain the enormous price premium attached to his paintings, sketches, and other work? Art historians may argue endlessly over this, but we provide an explanation of the huge price premium for works by Rembrandt and by other artistic superstars without assuming that the quality of their work is so much better than competitors.

The magnification of small differences in artistic quality into large differences in price is another source of superstars analyzed in a pioneering article by Rosen (1981). He emphasizes increasing returns or agglomeration effects, due to television, the Internet, and other low-cost methods of expanding markets for entertainers, athletes, and others that magnify the effects on earnings of small differences in their quality. Our analysis indicates that social markets also magnify small differences in quality, and produce a superstar phenomenon among artists and others, even without production economies of scale.

Assume a fixed number of objects in each of two classes of antiquities or other collectibles, A and B, such as paintings by the sixteenth-century Flemish artists Rembrandt and Vermeer, first editions of books by Adam Smith and David Hume, antique Persian and Chinese rugs, or rookie baseball cards of Mickey Mantle and Willie Mays. Following the discussion in the previous section, we also assume that an individual's willingness to pay for these collectibles depends not only on the characteristics of these objects but also on who owns them.

We simplify by assuming only two types of individuals, "leaders" (L) and "followers" (F). Pricing and sorting are trivial if the two classes of collectibles are close substitutes, and if L's want to own the same class of objects owned by other L's, while F's want to be in the same class as other F's. For then L's would tend to collect one class of objects and F's would collect another class, and the price differences between classes would be small. Large price differences between similar objects become possible when both L's and F's prefer the class of objects collected by L's. Therefore we assume that both L's and F's will pay more for an object when L's own relatively many of other objects in this class.

The analysis in Chapter 5 shows that equilibrium prices then depend not only on the attractiveness of the objects but also on the characteristics of who owns them. Indeed, equilibrium prices of objects in different classes may differ greatly even though everyone believes the objects in the different classes are equally attractive. For example, collectors may pay a lot more for Rembrandts than for Vermeers, even when Rembrandts are considered to be no better, because collectors of Rembrandts have much more prestige.

Figure 6.1 illustrates this phenomenon, where the vertical axis shows the ratio of prices that L's and F's are each willing to pay for, say, Van Goghs and Monets, while the proportion of owners of Van Goghs who are L's (s_a) is plotted along the horizontal axis. For simplicity of discussion, the number of Van Goghs is assumed to equal the number of Monets, and the total number of paintings equals the total number of collectors. The figure also assumes that both groups are willing to pay only a little more for Van Goghs than for Monets. Therefore, in competitive markets, the difference in the prices of paintings by these two

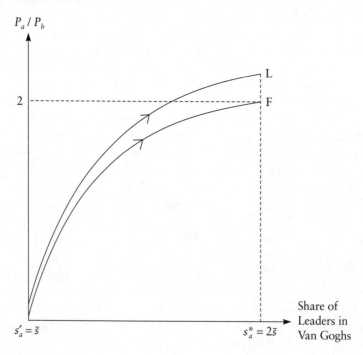

Figure 6.1

artists will also be very small if L's are equally likely to own them (if $s_a = s_b = \bar{s}$, the proportion of L's in the population of collectors).

However, since L's are assumed to have a greater relative preference for Van Goghs than F's do, they bid more for them when $s_a = \bar{s}$. As a result, the fraction of Van Goghs owned by L's rises, which increases the willingness to pay for Van Goghs of both L's and F's. Since the figure assumes that L's still want to own Van Goghs more than F's do as s_a increases, both s_a and P_a continue to rise until all the L's own Van Goghs—if the number of L's is less than the number of F's—and $s_a^* = 2\bar{s}$. In this segregated equilibrium, Van Goghs sell for over twice that of Monets, even though everyone only slightly prefers Van Goghs, because of the desire by both L's and F's to collect the same class of objects that L's collect—in this case Van Goghs.

The analysis illustrated by this example is developed more fully in Chapter 5 when discussing differences in housing prices between two neighborhoods. The general conclusion is that competition in social markets may magnify small differences in perceived quality among classes of objects into very large differences in equilibrium prices.

This conclusion implies, for example, that paintings by certain artists, or first editions of books by particular authors, may sell for many times those by others, even when "objective" differences in the quality of their work are not large. The reason is that the demand for work by certain artists and authors is sharply elevated because leaders collect their paintings and books. This increased demand greatly raises prices of works favored by leading collectors above prices of works that may only be slightly, if at all, inferior.

This analysis of the magnification of small differences in quality because of the desire to emulate leaders has special relevance to collecting because of the great difficulty in assessing the quality of many kinds of art, first editions, rugs, stamps, and other antiquities. It is not easy to determine definitively whether first editions of books by Adam Smith are "superior" to first editions by his close friend David Hume or by Parson Malthus, whether paintings by Van Gogh are superior to those by Cézanne or Monet, or whether baseball cards of Mickey Mantle are better than those of Ted Williams and Willie Mays.

Collectors often rely on expert opinion precisely because of these difficulties in assessing quality. But the frequent differences in opinion about quality even among acknowledged experts in a field means that collectors may also judge quality by the interests of leading collectors.

The many collectors who believe that objects demanded by leading collectors are of high quality bid up the prices of these objects. Then the high prices commanded by these objects help confirm that they are of high quality.

The fragility of assessments of differences in the qualities of competing paintings, books, antique rugs, pottery, and other collectibles implies that small shifts in opinion about quality by experts and leading collectors would be common, and even large shifts in opinion would not be rare. Yet our analysis of the effects of social markets implies that even small shifts in these assessments will have huge effects on prices, if the objects that improve in *perceived* quality begin to attract the leading collectors.

As it were, changes in the opinions of leading collectors toward even slightly favoring particular objects, perhaps induced by small changes in expert opinion, have multiplier effects on the demand for these objects. Changed opinions by leaders and experts might also change the opinions of followers, but the demands of followers for the class of objects now favored by leaders would increase even when the opinions of followers about quality did not change.

The demand for paintings by Van Gogh provides an apt illustration of the enormous effect of changes in opinion on the market value of an artist's work. Not a single one of his paintings sold during his lifetime, yet not very long after his death their value began to skyrocket. Perhaps this was mainly due to large changes in the opinions of art experts, but the enormous rise in the value of Van Gogh paintings would have occurred even with modest changes in expert opinion, once his work began to attract the attention of prominent collectors.

The magnification of even small perceived differences in qualities, combined with the difficulty of objectively assessing the relative qualities of works with different styles and from different times, implies that relative prices of art and other collectibles will fluctuate greatly over time as fashion and opinion change. This appears to be the case: prices of individual artists, and even prices for whole schools of artists, apparently have fluctuated greatly over time (see Frey and Pommerehne, 1989).

The instability of preferences about different artists is probably stronger for contemporary artists than for earlier artists, because the emphasis now is more on novelty and less on accumulated artistic skills. This is Galenson and Weinberg's (2000) conclusion from evidence that the most expensive paintings by prominent twentieth-century artists were generally produced at much younger ages than the most valuable paintings by masters from earlier centuries, even though these masters did not live as long.

4. Copies and Forgeries

Forgers and unscrupulous dealers have an incentive to misrepresent particular objects as belonging to a class of objects that sell for a great deal since few persons can tell the difference between originals and excellent copies, or between originals and those produced by lesser knowns. For example, even many collectors of Japanese Ukiyoe woodblock prints cannot tell the difference between prints by the great nineteenth-century artist Ando Hiroshige and excellent copies of his work, or between Hiroshiges and prints by some of his contemporaries.

The high price of some originals explains why markets for old paintings, pottery, and other collectibles are plagued by forgeries and fakes since they can usually be produced at a fraction of the cost of expensive originals. Some experts even specialize in detecting fakes, although even the greatest experts have sometimes been fooled by excellent fakes.

Most collectors are hurt by an increased supply of forgeries, for that lowers the prices of the original objects that are substitutes for the forgeries. Moreover, forgeries make it more difficult to separate the demands of leaders, which further reduces prices. When forgeries of particular objects become too common, demand will shift to other objects that have fewer forgeries.

A good example is what happened to the demand for leather jackets in the United States. Initially these jackets were a prestige item among young people, because they signified rebellion and being "cool." Although competitively produced, they were expensive since they were made of costly lambskin or calfskin. Before long, however, leather jackets made of much cheaper pigskin and goatskin were imported and sold at much lower prices. Since most people cannot tell whether a person is wearing a calfskin or lambskin leather jacket rather than a "forgery," leather jackets began to lose their appeal and prestige (see *Wall Street Journal*, 1994, p. B1).

Another interesting example began with a request by *Miami Vice*, a highly successful television program of the 1980s, for a car that looked exactly like a Ferrari Daytona Spyder but was much cheaper to make. Spyders then retailed for $1 million to $2 million because they were produced in very limited editions, which created an image of exclusivity. Capitalizing on the popularity of the show, the producer of the bogus car then went into business selling cars that looked exactly like Spyders, but had frames bolted on the undercarriage of ordinary cars. Although he was above board about what he was selling, these "copies" had a market because it appeared to *others* that their owners were driving expensive and prestigious cars.

The Ferrari company claimed that the producer was infringing on its trademark because most people who saw the copies could not tell whether they were the real thing. A federal court of appeals upheld Ferrari's claim that these cars created a misleading impression for observers, and forced the producer out of business (see Ferrari S.p.A. v. Roberts, 1991).

This example illustrates that there may be financial incentives to copy not only antiques but also trademarked goods that sell for much above their cost of production. Fashion houses like Valentino and Estrada, and Swiss watchmakers like Rolex and Patek Phillippe, are continually trying to detect and eliminate much cheaper copies that are falsely represented as originals. Cartier alone is said to spend more than $7 million each year combating counterfeits (see *Financial Times*, 1998, p. II). Chapter 7 considers the role of trademarked goods in segregating demands of leaders.

Our discussion has presumed that even excellent and hard to detect copies and forgeries are much less desired than originals. Yet if few owners, and even fewer of those who view an object, can distinguish originals from excellent copies, why should copies sell for so much less than originals, especially when originals are generally in poorer condition? For example, a first edition in good condition of Adam Smith's *Wealth of Nations* sells for over $50,000, while a German publisher sells high-quality limited edition exact replicas of this edition for about $1,000.

Veblen recognized the huge difference in price between excellent copies and originals: "It appears that (1) while the different materials of which the two spoons are made each possesses beauty and serviceability for the purpose for which it is used, the material of the hand-wrought spoon is some one hundred times more valuable than the baser metal, without very greatly excelling the later in intrinsic beauty of grain or colour, and without being in any appreciable degree superior in point of mechanical serviceability; (2) if a close inspection should show that the supposed hand-wrought spoon were in reality only a very clever imitation of hand-wrought goods, but an imitation so cleverly wrought as to give the same impression of line and surface to any but minute examination by a trained eye, the utility of the article, including the gratification which the user derives from its contemplation as an object of beauty, would immediately decline by some eighty or ninety per cent, or even more" (1934, pp. 127–128).

We recognize that collectors may be willing to pay a great deal for the mental image that an object, such as a painting or piece of sculpture, was produced long ago by an outstanding artist rather than by some nameless imitator. However, this explanation of the large price premium between originals and copies does not explain the value placed on first editions. Adam Smith and other authors of editions that sell for a large amount did not print the books but used commercial publishers. Moreover, is the value placed on the mental image of major artists who are personally crafting their works enough to explain why originals often sell for more than a hundred times that of outstanding copies?

Perhaps, but it is not necessary to believe that the value placed on such images and related considerations is responsible for all, or even most, of the huge premium placed on originals. For the analysis of social markets explains these premiums even without assuming *any* preference for originals over copies. This explanation relies on the fundamental difference between the supply of originals and copies. While the supply of original first editions, old stamps, paintings, and other collectibles is more or less fixed, copies can usually be cheaply produced in large quantities. This means that copies *cannot* sell for more than their cost of production, regardless of demand, whereas originals can command a very high price without inducing additional production.

Therefore, markets can only separate leaders from followers by bidding up the prices of originals, *even if neither leaders nor followers prefer originals to copies.* This interpretation only requires that both leaders and followers much prefer to collect the same class of objects that leaders collect, and that copies and originals can be distinguished.

Under these conditions, copies cannot sell for more than originals because prices of copies are pinned down by the low cost of production. The *only* possible separating equilibrium is for originals to be more expensive. And they can be *much* more expensive even if the demand to be with leaders is only moderately powerful.

Social Markets and the Escalation of Quality: The World of Veblen Revisited

(with Edward Glaeser)

1. Introduction

The discussion in Chapter 6 of price differences between famous works of art and excellent copies shows the importance of supply conditions when other collectors want to own the same class of objects owned by leading collectors and other elite groups. Elites cannot use price to separate their consumption from that of others in competitive markets with supply augmentable at more or less constant costs, for these costs pin down long-run prices. Supply conditions crucially affect the operation of social markets, yet supply conditions have been largely neglected in discussions of social influences on behavior.

Segregation of leaders and followers might be possible in competitive markets if leaders and followers have very different tastes, for then leaders might consume one set of goods and followers a different set. For example, if leaders have much a greater preference for higher-quality goods than do followers, leaders might consume higher-quality while followers consume cheaper lower-quality goods. However, even rather large differences in tastes for quality might not be sufficient to segregate their choices if followers wanted to buy qualities similar to those bought by leaders.

Conversely, the qualities consumed by leaders and followers might differ even when they have exactly the same preferences for quality, if leaders have a stronger preference than followers to consume the same class of goods as other leaders. In that case, leaders may consume more expensive goods than followers only to separate their consumption from followers. Indeed, we will show in this chapter that leaders may be forced to absurdly high qualities in order to separate themselves from followers.

2. Social Demand for High-Quality Goods

Entrepreneurs always try to find goods that appeal to consumers. However, they would have special incentives to discover goods that appeal much more to leaders than to followers if leaders and followers would pay a lot for goods that are mainly consumed by other leaders. In particular, it may be easy to find qualities of goods that appeal much more to leaders, since leaders and followers tend to have different incomes, education, age, and other personal characteristics that lead them to prefer different qualities of many goods. Moreover, qualities can differ in almost limitless varieties including leather instead of vinyl car seats, handmade watches with gold and fine diamonds, port aged for more than fifty years, dresses made with silk rather than wool, houses with 30,000 or more square feet of space, and the ability to avoid flying "commercial" by owning private jets.

Entrepreneurs choose the qualities that attract consumers subject to the profit constraint that prices must at least cover costs of production. This section analyzes the choice of qualities in social markets with constant costs and free entry. Therefore, the equilibrium price of each quality produced would equal its cost of production. If the cost of quality, q, is $c(q)$, the competitive price of q is determined by

$$(7.1) \qquad\qquad p(q) = c(q),$$

where it is assumed that $c' > 0$ and $c'' > 0$. In Figure 7.1, the convex curve CC represents this relation between cost and quality.

Each consumer is assumed to buy one unit of this product, and is free to choose the quality desired. Utility depends on quality, its market price, and also on the characteristics of others who buy the same quality. We assume again in this chapter that consumers are divided into only two homogeneous groups, L and F, and that both groups prefer to consume the same qualities as L's. The surplus to each consumer, or willingness to pay for each quality, net of the price of quality, is as-

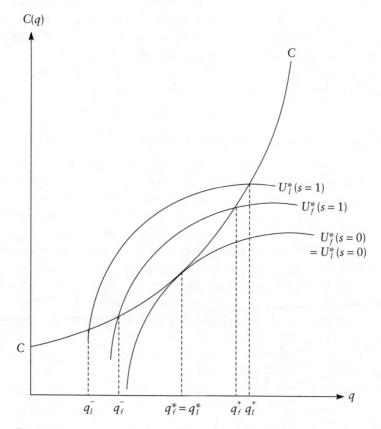

Figure 7.1

sumed to be separable in quality and the proportion of consumers of that quality who are L's.

$$(7.2) \qquad\qquad U_f = V(q) + s(q) - p(q)$$

$$(7.3) \qquad\qquad U_l = aV(q) + bs(q) - p(q).$$

The function V is increasing and concave, the fraction of consumers who are L's, s, is bounded between 0 and 1, and a and b are positive parameters. The assumption that s enters linearly in these equations is a simplification of little importance.

Each L and F chooses the quality that maximizes utility in (7.2) or

(7.3), subject to the competitive equilibrium condition in equation (7.1) and subject to the market values of s for different qualities. The feasible market separating or pooling equilibria in s depends on the convexity of the cost function, and the parameters a and b of these utility functions.

If $a = b = 1$, preferences of L's and F's for both quality and peers are identical, and the behavior of L's and F's cannot be separated in competitive equilibrium. There would be integration, or a pooling equilibrium, with quality determined from the same FOC for each F and L:

$$(7.4) \qquad V'(q_f^*) = c'(q_f^*) \quad \text{and} \quad V'(q_l^*) = c'(q_l^*),$$

with $q_l^* = q_f^* = q^*$ and $s(q^*) = \bar{s}$, where $\bar{s}$ is the ratio of all L's to all consumers. (All results in this chapter are proved more rigorously in the appendix to this chapter.)

Therefore, for separating equilibria to be possible, L's and F's must differ either in their tastes for quality ($a \neq 1$) or their tastes to be with leaders ($b \neq 1$). To show how separating equilibrium emerge, start with $a = 1$, so that L and F place the same values on differences in quality, but now assume that $b > 1$. This implies that L's are willing to pay more than F's for better "peers"—that is, to consume the same quality that L's consume. There is still an integrated equilibrium, where all L's and F's would choose the quality given by the FOCs in equation (7.4). But the discussion in Chapters 5 and 6 shows why this integration or pooling would not be stable when $b > 1$, since L's are willing to pay more to be with other L's than F's are.

In a fully separating equilibrium, all F's consume one quality, all L's choose another, and no one wants to change her quality. If F's are separated and do not want to change, they will choose the quality that maximizes their utility, given by q_f^* in equation (7.4), which yields a utility of U_f^*. In Figure 7.1, a concave indifference curve of F, $U_f^*(s = 0)$, is tangent to the cost curve CC at quality q^*. Assuming a sufficient range for $V(q) - c(q)$, there exist two quality levels when $s = 1$—one above and one below q_f^*—that provide the same utility to F's as U_f^*:

$$(7.5) \qquad U_f^*(s = 1) = U_f^*(s = 0) = V(q_f^-) + 1 - c(q_f^-) = V(q_f^+) + 1 - c(q_f^+),$$

$$\text{where } q_f^- < q_f^* = q_l^* = q^* < q_f^+.$$

The indifference curve with $s = 1$, $U_f^*(s = 1)$ that gives the same utility as $U_f^*(s = 0)$ is shown in Figure 7.1 to intersect CC at both q_f^+ and q_f^-. $U_f^*(s = 1)$ lies above $U_f^*(s = 0)$ because the increase in utility as s goes from 0 to 1 must be offset by a sufficient increase in the cost of different qualities. Since $U_f^*(s = 0)$ is tangent to CC, the higher indifference curve $U_f^*(s = 1)$ intersects CC both above and below q^*.

Clearly, if L's simply maximized utility, independently of the values of s, they would choose $q^* = q_l^* = q_f^*$. But since F's also choose that quality, it would be an integrating, not a separating, outcome. Suppose, however, that only F's choose q^*. Then $s = 0$ at that quality, and if one L wanted to choose the same quality as the F's, it would get the utility U_l^*. The indifference curve that gives L's the same utility as U_l^* when $s = 1$ would lie above $U_l^*(s = 0)$ since an increase in s raises L's utility— see the indifference curve $U_l^*(s = 1)$ in Figure 7.1. Since by assumption, L's place more weight than F's on having prestigious peers, $U_l^*(s = 1)$ also lies above $U_f^*(s = 1)$. Hence $U_l^*(s = 1)$ intersects CC at the two points, $q_l^+ > q_f^+$ and $q_l^- < q_f^-$.

The equilibrium choice of quality by F's and L's will be stable and separating as long as L's choose a quality between either q_l^- and q_f^+, or q_l^- and q_f^-. Even though an F could increase s from 0 to 1 by defecting to the higher quality chosen by L's, that quality would be so high that it would lower utility compared with $U_f^*(s = 0)$. Similarly an L does not want to defect to q^* because the reduction in s would reduce utility by more than it would be increased by L's having a more optimal quality (at q^*).

Within the interval between q_l^+ and q_f^+, each L has an incentive to defect to the lower boundary q_f^+ since that would not reduce s below 1, and yet would raise L's utility—move L to a lower indifference curve. Similarly, within the interval between q_l^- and q_f^-, each L has an incentive to defect to the upper boundary q_f^- since that would not lower s below 1, and would raises L's utility. So, in this case, the only stable equilibria are separating, and they have all F's consuming q_f^* and all L's consuming either q_f^- or q_f^+ since neither an L nor an F would then want to change qualities (see the appendix for a more formal discussion of this equilibrium based on the Cho and Kreps, 1987, stability refinement criterion).

Note that in these separating equilibria, the F's maximize their utility and choose their optimal qualities. However, the L's are not maximizing their utility assuming that s is fixed at $s = 1$ since they would then choose q_l^* rather than either q_f^- or q_f^+. Each L is faced with the choice between q_l^* with $s = 0$, and either q_f^- or q_f^+ with $s = 1$. They choose the latter because that gives greater utility.

The stronger the utility to F's from better peers, the larger must be the equilibrium quality difference to discourage F's from buying the same quality products as L's. This forces L's to consume a sufficiently higher or lower quality that prevents F's from copying them. Therefore, when social considerations are important, L's may be forced far away from their optimal quality even though they may only have a very slightly stronger preference to have prestigious peers than F's do.

A similar analysis applies if L's and F's have the same preferences for peers, but have different preferences for qualities. Suppose that $b = 1$, and that L's have a greater preference for higher quality, so that $a > 1$. The optimal quality chosen by L's independently of social considerations would be given by the FOC

(7.6)
$$aV'(q_l^*) = c'(q_l^*), \qquad q_l^* > q_f^*.$$

In this case, L's strictly prefer q_f^+ to q_f^- in Figure 7.1 since higher quality gives them greater utility.

If the L's preference for better quality—measured by a—is sufficiently large that $q_l^* > q_f^+$, L would then choose q_l^*, F would choose q_f^*, and the equilibrium would again be fully separating. This is shown in Figure 7.2, where q_l^* with $s = 1$ is on a higher indifference curve of F, or provides lower utility, than $U_f^*(s = 1)$. Moreover, it is clear from this figure that q_f^* with $s = 0$ gives L's less utility that q_l^* with $s = 1$.

If, on the other hand, $q_l^* < q_f^+$, either there is a fully separating equilibrium where L's choose q_f^+ and F's choose q_f^*, or there is a pooling (or semipooling) equilibrium at a value of q between q_f^* and q_f^+.

When L's and F's have the same taste for quality ($a = 1$), but F's prefer better peers more than L's do ($b < 1$), the only stable equilibrium is fully integrating and pooling at the same optimal quality for both L's and F's (q^*). More generally, stable pooling or semipooling equilibria only exist when $a > b$ and $1 \geq b$, and the pooling equilibrium quality ($\hat{q}$) is defined by the equation $c'(\hat{q})/V'(\hat{q}) = (a - b)/(1 - b)$ (see the appendix for the derivation of this equation, and for other results on the kinds of equilibria possible with different values of a and b).

Whether L's or F's have greater preference to be with more prestigious peers (whether $b \gtrless 1$) is a property of preferences for which our analysis provides a couple of important insights. If leaders are

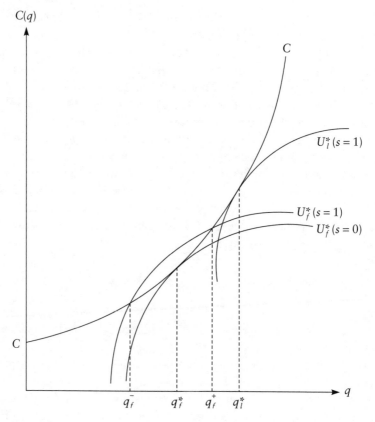

Figure 7.2

richer than followers, as is usually the case, a positive income effect for the "quality" of peers implies that leaders would be willing to pay more than followers to have more prestigious peers. Yet, as we have seen, a greater preference to have prestigious peers does not per se imply that leaders consume higher-quality products, since separating equilibria exist with leaders consuming lower, as well as higher, qualities than followers.

However, if leaders are richer than followers they will also have a positive income effect for quality of goods. The evidence strongly indicates that leaders typically consume higher-quality goods and objects, often much higher, than most followers. For example, rich fashion leaders wear designer clothes while followers tend to wear copies, and leading collectors have antique rugs and prime first editions, while followers tend to have recently produced rugs and later editions.

But sometimes "leaders" are poorer and may consume lower-quality goods than followers. For example, some "in" restaurants cater to young people and try to "ration" out the rich by refusing to take reservations, so that diners must spend considerable time queuing for tables. Some clothing fashions originated among African Americans in the inner city and spread to wealthier individuals who may consume more expensive versions of the fashionable clothing.

Moreover, differences in preferences for quality depend not only on income and other group differences but also on markets and incentives. Entrepreneurs can raise their profits if they discover products, including different qualities, that appeal to L's more than to F's. The reason is that L's are willing to pay more, perhaps much more, for products that separate their demands from those of F's.

Since L's and F's are distinct groups that differ in various personal and demographic characteristics, and since entrepreneurs can choose over an infinite number of qualities, many dimensions of quality are likely to separate the preferences of L's and F's. All that is needed are clever and innovative entrepreneurs to find them. Note that the differences in preferences for quality between L's and F's discovered and highlighted by market forces may not be typical of numerous types of quality that are not produced and sold because preferences of leaders and followers for these qualities are similar.

We have shown, moreover, that entrepreneurs need not discover quality dimensions over which L's and F's have very different tastes. For leaders consume much higher quality merchandise than followers even when they have only slightly stronger preference for better quality than followers do—that is, even when a in equation (7.3) is only slightly above 1.

Some of this discussion is analytically similar to the literature on monopoly pricing that discriminates among classes of consumers by producing goods of different qualities (see Mussa and Rosen, 1978; Tirole, 1988). But a couple of major differences distinguish quality in social and monopolistic markets. Price discrimination always requires monopoly pricing, whereas leaders and followers may consume different qualities even in perfectly competitive markets. Price discrimination also requires different groups to have different willingness to pay for higher-quality goods, whereas in social markets leaders and followers may consume different qualities even when they have the same willingness to pay for higher quality. Leaders may pay much more for higher-quality goods than followers only because other leaders are consuming these goods.

Our analysis is analytically even closer to the "signaling" literature (see also Chapter 5, section 5). In those discussions, "lower" types try to give the impression to firms and others that they are "higher" types by obtaining the same education or other observable characteristics as higher types, whereas the higher types try to differentiate their schooling and so on from that of lower types. However, our analysis does not necessarily assume that both types prefer to consume the same quality goods as higher types in order to provide signals about their types. Types may be known by everyone, so that many other reasons might explain why both types prefer to consume the same qualities as high types. But the analytical implications of social behavior—whatever the motivation—are frequently similar to those of signaling behavior, as in this discussion of quality escalation by leaders.

3. Escalated Qualities and Efficiency

The separating equilibria derived in the last section are generally not efficient. L's would be better off and F's would be no worse off if F's did not change their quality, while L's chose the quality that maximizes their utility when $s = 1$. For example, if $a = 1$ and b is only a little above 1, L's optimal q will be only a little above F's quality, q^*, if L's do not have to worry about the effects of their choice on F's choice of quality. If F's continue to choose q^*, the F's are no worse off than at the competitive separating equilibrium and the L's are all better off if they consume a quality that is only a little higher than q^*.

In competitive equilibrium, however, the L's cannot succeed in separating their consumption by choosing a quality only a little above q^*. For if they did that, F's would then also choose to consume a little higher quality, and the equilibrium would be fully integrated (but not stable). To escape the F's, the L's are forced to consume a high enough quality (q_f^+ in Figure 7.1) to discourage the F's from following them.

There are many examples of quality being chased up the ladder to outlandishly expensive levels in order to give distinction, although what is "outlandish" can be debated, and what is "distinction" is mainly in the eyes of the beholder and his or her peers. Examples include Bar Mitzvah parties for thirteen-year-olds that cost over $100,000, diamond rings that sell for over $50,000, watches that cost in six figures (*Financial Times*, 1998), skyboxes at sporting events that rent for $150,000 per year, personal trainers and massage therapists, suitcases that cost more than $2,000, designer women's suits that sell for $20,000, very expensive vodkas that are just as tasteless as cheap vodkas, automobiles that cost a half-million dollars, and tearing down homes with a "mere" 10,000 square feet to build "trophy" homes with 40,000 square feet and more—see the amusing discussion of the foibles of the rich on Long Island by Nussbaum (1998).

Developers of neighborhoods may try to attract only rich, young, or other clientele by offering amenities that appeal to these groups and not to groups they want to keep out. A developer may build elaborate golfing facilities that appeal to rich families or "state of the art" athletic and social facilities to appeal to young singles. The "appeal" is partly that others are not willing to pay so much for these facilities since the value of amenities to particular groups depends not only on how they value them but also on how they are valued by others. Chapter 5 shows that communities may spend a lot on schools, swimming pools, and other luxury facilities in order to raise taxes and property values beyond the means of unwanted groups.

Veblen repeatedly draws attention to what he considers the waste that arises from the desire for distinction: "a code of accredited canons of consumption . . . is to hold the consumer up to a standard of expensiveness and wastefulness in the consumption of goods and in his employment of time and effort" (1934, p. 116).

We have shown that the separating equilibria that result from competition are not efficient; separating equilibria may be less efficient than pooling or partially pooling equilibria. The reason is that equilibrium prices of goods in competitive markets do not fully incorporate the desires of both followers and leaders to have leaders as peers. Fully applicable here is Proposition 5.1, which proves a general tendency for competition to produce excessive levels of segregation between leaders and their followers.

When the competitive equilibrium in social markets is not efficient, everyone could be made better off if governments interfered in choices, either to encourage greater integration or to prevent followers from copying leaders as they moved up the quality ladder. Laws during the Middle Ages did forbid commoners from wearing the same clothing as nobility (see Tuchman, 1978), and colonial laws in Massachusetts regulated everyone's clothing toward simplicity.

Frequently, however, governments discourage integration not to improve efficiency but to promote the interests of powerful political groups. Clearly, the sumptuary laws of the Middle Ages were instigated by the nobility to help them maintain their distinctiveness. Another example is that until the second half of this century state and local governments in the southern part of the United States segregated schools and other facilities by race and tried explicitly to segregate housing in order to promote the interests of whites (see Cutler, Glaeser, and Vidgor, 1999).

4. Trademarks and Copyrights

Producers want to differentiate their products from those of competitors through trademarking and advertising since that allows them to raise prices without attracting competition. These private advantages of trademarked goods are so obvious and pervasive that some efficiency advantages of trademarks have been ignored (although see the brief discussions of social effects in Higgins and Rubin, 1986, and Landes and Posner, 1987).

Producers in social markets have an additional and often powerful incentive to differentiate their products through trademarking if that separates leaders from followers. For leaders might be willing to pay a lot for a product consumed mainly by the other leaders, especially if they do not have to consume excessively high qualities. Trademarks and advertising may give producers the power to raise prices sufficiently above that of physically comparable products in order to keep out followers.

Economists have usually been hostile to trademarked goods, and have been puzzled by their power to attract customers, since they are often expensive but may not greatly differ from much cheaper goods. Calvin Klein jeans, Ferrari cars, Chanel suits, Givenchy perfumes, and Starbuck's coffees are just a sampling of prestigious trademarked goods that have differentiated markets, even though material differences between these goods and much cheaper competitors are not large.

These and other examples of high-priced prestige goods would, indeed, be puzzling if consumers were only interested in material characteristics. Such a presumption, however, ignores the critical importance of social considerations. Trademarked goods may not be materially special, but trademarking may help control the identity of consumers.

For example, that Chanel ladies' suits are not much "better" than good copies is unimportant to many women who buy Chanels. What is crucial to them is that the "right" women wear Chanels. The utility of wearing an expensive Chanel suit depends not so much on whether it is sufficiently better made than much cheaper suits, but on the aura connected with Chanel, partly related to who else wears these suits.

These social aspects of consumption explain why these companies with prestigious names may be profitable, despite the availability of much cheaper, materially similar goods.

To increase demand by elite consumers, producers try to prevent consuming by others, even though that appears to be irrational because it apparently reduces demand. Producers may only advertise in magazines and television programs that are read or watched mainly by elites. They may directly ration sales if they can successfully keep out "less desirable" consumers, or they may indirectly ration by refusing to sell to distributors who cater mainly to the hoi polloi.

Levi Strauss preferred to sell Levi's in its own stores, so that its market would not be reduced by the sale of "imitation" and cheaper jeans in the same shops. But until recent years an antitrust ruling prevented the company from having its own stores in the United States.

Exclusive perfumes and other prestigious personal care items are usually distributed in expensive department stores. Givenchy objected when discount stores started to sell its perfume Amarige, even though initially that would have increased Amarige's market. Givenchy claimed mass distribution would damage the elite image of Amarige because that would considerably reduce its appearance of exclusivity. Givenchy litigated and the courts decided in its favor (*New York Times,* 1993b, p. 37). A young Iranian woman successfully launched a nail polish company by selling exotic colors. Since image was so important, she refused lucrative offers for much wider distribution.

A more direct approach to attracting elites is through price discrimination, for companies could charge desired customers sufficiently lower prices that would internalize the positive effects of their consumption on demands by others. Such price discrimination could even be efficiency improving if it gave followers access to prestige goods by forcing them to pay for negative spillovers of their consumption on the demands of both followers and leaders.

However, rationing and price discrimination are sometimes illegal, or they are not feasible when producers cannot distinguish followers from leaders. But if leaders are willing to pay more than followers for prestigious trademarked goods than followers, demands can be separated by sufficient increases in price to all consumers.

Figure 7.3 gives one possible scenario, where the horizontal curve CC gives marginal and average production costs of a differentiated good in a social market, and DD is the aggregate demand of both followers and leaders. We assume that mainly leaders consume this good at high prices (the share of leaders, s, is high then), and that followers

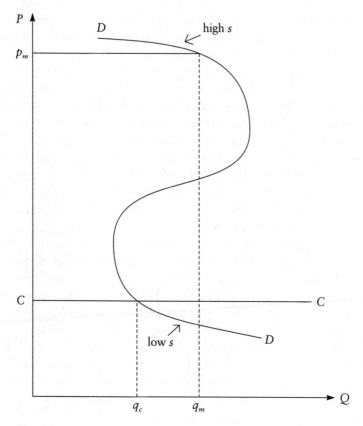

Figure 7.3

are more price sensitive so that they increase their relative demand (s falls) as price falls. Since both leaders and followers want to consume the same goods as leaders, a fall in s reduces demands of both leaders and followers. This negative effect on demand of increased relative consumption by followers reduces the price elasticity of the aggregate demand curve as price falls.

Indeed Figure 7.3 assumes that demand is actually positively sloped in one interval because the negative effect on quantity demanded of the fall in s, in this interval, dominates the positive effect on demand of lower prices. This positively sloped interval is surrounded by two more "normal" intervals where demand is negatively related to price. At high prices mainly leaders consume the good; at low prices mainly followers do.

The competitive equilibrium would be along the cost function, where price equals C; in this example, demand comes mainly from followers. If trademarks help differentiate goods, price rises above the competitive level, but in this case the composition of consumers also shifts toward leaders. The optimal monopoly price is assumed to be at p_m, well above the competitive price of C, because demand is positively related to price in much of the interval between these prices. At the monopoly price, most consumers are leaders because others are priced out of this market.

In this example, total consumption at the high monopoly price is actually *greater* than at the much lower competitive price. This is one important difference between social and regular markets, and helps explain the seemingly strange behavior of Givenchy and other companies that appear to restrict sales of their products.

Critics often pan highly promoted perfumes, clothing, jewelry, cars, and other products that sell for much more than competing goods yet even though their materials and even workmanship are not substantially better than cheaper imitations. They are right that the high prices are not explained by materialistic qualities, but they are wrong when they infer that heavy promotion misleads consumers into overpaying for these products.

Consumers are largely paying for image, prestige, and distinctiveness, which are social rather than material characteristics of certain products. Veblen observed with considerable insight that as societies become wealthier, consumers have the luxury of changing their concerns from physical comfort and basic necessities to "the esteem and envy of one's fellow men" (1934, p. 32).

Although competitive equilibria for traditional goods tend to satisfy consumer preferences efficiently, competitive outcomes in social markets tend to be inefficient. We have shown earlier in this chapter that leaders end up consuming excessively high quality merchandise in competitive markets in order to be separated from other consumers.

Trademarking and promotion may greatly raise the price of a product because a higher price mostly attracts leaders, as at the price p_m in Figure 7.3. Paying a monopoly price for trademarked goods is then a possible attractive alternative for leaders to paying competitive prices for much higher quality goods.

Therefore, that many expensive trademarked goods are not greatly superior in materials and workmanship to cheaper competitors could be efficiency raising rather than lowering. These trademarked goods may help avoid the escalation of quality as leaders try to separate from followers. In other words, heavily promoted exclusive trademarked goods may contribute to greater efficiency precisely because they do not have such high-quality materials and workmanship. Leaders as well as producers often prefer monopolized trademarked products of good quality to more expensive, higher-quality products that are competitively priced.

Such trademarked goods are, in effect, promises to maintain a limited and exclusive clientele. Yet owners of trademarked names with great recognition value may be tempted to violate their implicit commitments to exclusivity in order to profit from marketing an expanded array of merchandise under their name. These extensions of scope of a name are sometimes highly successful, as when Ralph Lauren developed the Polo brand of apparel, Hermes marketed ties and scarves to supplement its famous handbags, and Cartier developed the cheaper tank watch for Americans.

But extensions of trademarks are delicate, and it is easy to go too far and lose the commitment to exclusivity. Indeed, cheaper versions of deluxe products can even kill the markets for deluxe brands because they no longer are identified with exclusivity. Gucci gave its name to so many products that the name for a while lost most of its value as signifying exclusivity (see the discussion in *The Economist*, 1992b, pp. 95–98).

Counterfeiting and copying may also destroy the market for high-priced trademarked goods because they lead to apparently similar goods at much lower prices that attract followers. Italian fashion houses like Prada are plagued by much cheaper counterfeits, sometimes produced in the very same shops that supply the originals.

Copies that are not misrepresented as originals may still find a market among followers and others who may not care whether they have the "real thing." For example, they may be interested in whether other consumers believe they have exclusive expensive goods—see the discussion of copies in Chapter 6.

But no matter what attracts consumers to copies and counterfeits, the greater their similarity to trademarked originals, the greater the difficulty in maintaining markets for the originals. Look-alikes can greatly dilute the exclusivity conveyed by trademarked goods, which explains the lawsuits and other efforts by owners of valuable trademarks to put counterfeiters and copiers out of business.

Chanel successfully brought a lawsuit against a perfume maker who advertised that the smell of its perfume could not be distinguished from that of Chanel No. Five (see Smith v. Chanel, Inc., 1968). Lacoste opposed the sale of its shirts in discount outlets unless the famous alligator insignia was removed. The French champagne industry has been highly profitable partly because other sparkling wine producers cannot label their products as "champagne" (see Flanders and Thiry, 1991). Chapter 6 discussed the successful lawsuit by Ferrari to prevent the sale of cars that on the outside looked exactly like its very expensive Spyder, but had much cheaper parts inside.

Appendix 7A

Assumptions Followers maximize $V(q) + s(q) - C(q)$, where q is quality, $s(q)$ is the proportion of the good's consumers who are leaders, $V(.)$ is a twice-differentiable, increasing concave function, and $C(.)$ is a twice-differentiable, increasing convex function. Leaders maximize $\alpha V(q) + \beta s(q) - C(q)$, where α and β are constants. The function $s(q)$ equals the realized proportion of leaders and followers consuming the good when the good is being consumed in equilibrium. When a quality level is not being consumed in equilibrium, then this function must reflect beliefs about off-the-equilibrium-path actions. To determine the value of $s(q)$ for these off-the-equilibrium-path actions, we use the following stability refinement.

Definition of Stability (based on Cho and Kreps, 1987, p. D1) Let $\tilde{S}_F(q)$ denote the level of s that would induce a follower to deviate to q and let $\tilde{S}_L(q)$ denote the level of s that would induce a leader to deviate to q. Intuitively when $\tilde{S}_L(q) > \tilde{S}_F(q)$, it is harder to induce a leader to deviate to q than to induce a follower to do so. An equilibrium set of beliefs is stable if, for values of q that are not played in equilibrium, $s(q) = 1$ if $\tilde{S}_F(q) > \tilde{S}_L(q)$ and $s(q) = 0$ if $\tilde{S}_L(q) > \tilde{S}_F(q)$. The stability refinement ensures that people believe that off-the-equilibrium-path actions are more likely to come from the players who have the greater incentive to take those actions.

Definitions of Terms Used in Proposition 7.1 We let q_f^* solve $V'(q_F^*)$ $= C'(q_F^*), U_F^* = V(q_F^*) - C(q_F^*)$, and q_L^* solves $\alpha V'(q_L^*) = C'(q_L^*)$. For q

$> q_F^*$, $V(q) - C(q)$ is monotonically decreasing, continuous, and by assumption $\lim_{q \to \infty} V(q) - C(q) = -\infty$, there exists a value of $q > q_F^*$, denoted q_F^+ such that $U_F^* - 1 = V(q_F^+) - C(q_F^+)$. Likewise, for $q < q_F^*$, $V(q) - C(q)$ is monotonically increasing, continuous, and by assumption $\lim_{q \to 0} V(q) - C(q) = -\infty$, so there must also exist a value of $q < q_F^*$, denoted q_F^- such that $U_F^* - 1 = V(q_F^-) - C(q_F^-)$. We also denote $\hat{q}$ to solve

$$\frac{C'(\hat{q})}{V'(\hat{q})} = \frac{\alpha - \beta}{1 - \beta}.$$

We first state the main proposition of this appendix in several parts, and then prove three lemmas that help prove this proposition.

Proposition 7.1   If $q_L^* > q_F^+$ or $q_F^- > q_L^*$, then a unique stable equilibrium exists where leaders choose q_L^* and followers choose q_F^*. When $q_F^+ > q_L^* > q_F^-$, if $\beta > \alpha$, or $\beta > 1$, or $\hat{q} > q_F^+$ or $q_F^- > \hat{q}$, then a unique stable equilibrium exists where followers choose q_F^* and leaders choose q_F^- if $1 > \alpha$ or q_F^+ if $\alpha > 1$. If $\alpha > \beta$, $1 > \beta$ and $q_F^+ > \hat{q} > q_F^-$, then a unique stable equilibrium exists where all leaders and some followers consume $\hat{q}$, and other followers consume q_F^*

Lemma 1   In all separating equilibria, followers choose q_F^*.

In a separating equilibrium, followers are choosing a quality level not being consumed by any leaders, and, as such, the only quality level that maximizes their utility is q_F^*.

Lemma 2   In all separating equilibria when $q_F^+ > q_L^* > q_F^-$, leaders choose q_F^+ if $\alpha > 1$ or q_F^- if $\alpha < 1$.

In a separating equilibrium if leaders choose a value of q between q_F^+ and q_F^-, then followers will also choose that value of q (because they will prefer this to their equilibrium outcome). If leaders choose a value of q greater than q_F^+, then consider a deviation of a leader to a value $(q + q_F^+)/2$. The level of s needed to make a follower indifferent between $(q + q_F^+)/2$ and q_F^* is greater than one. The level of s needed to make a leader indifferent between $(q + q_F^+)/2$ and q is less than one because $(q + q_F^+)/2$ is closer to q_L^* than q is. As such $s((q + q_F^+)/2) = 1$, and the leaders will defect to $(q + q_F^+)/2$. This reasoning is symmetric, so you cannot have a separating equilibrium where $q < q_F^-$. The stability refinement ensures that $s(q_F^+) = s(q_F^-) = 1$, so the leaders will choose q_F^+ if and only if $\alpha V(q_F^+) + \beta s(q_F^+) - C(q_F^+) > \alpha V(q_F^-) + \beta s(q_F^-) - C(q_F^-)$ or $\alpha > 1$ (as $V(q_F^+) - C(q_F^+) = V(q_F^-) - C(q_F^-)$).

Lemma 3   Pooling equilibria can only exist at the point $\hat{q}$, when $\alpha > \beta$ and $1 > \beta$. All followers who are not at the pooling point will consume q_F^*.

Generically, there cannot be pooling at two points—the differences in $s(q)$ between the two points cannot make both leaders and followers indifferent between the two points. All followers who are not at the pooling point will consume q_F^*, because there is no reason for them not to be at their ideal consumption level. Define

$$B(q) = \tilde{s}_L(q) - \tilde{s}_F(q) = \frac{U_L - \beta U_F}{\beta} + \frac{1 - \beta}{\beta} C(q) - \frac{\alpha - \beta}{\beta} V(q),$$

where $U_{L,F}$ is the equilibrium payoff for each type. By the stability refinement when $B(q) > 0$, then $s(q) = 1$ (for q's not consumed in equilibrium), and when $B(q) < 0$, then $s(q) = 1$. Given the existence of a quality level q' consumed by both leaders and followers (a pooling equilibrium), then

$$B(q) = \frac{\alpha - \beta}{\beta}(V(q)') - V(q)) - \frac{1 - \beta}{\beta}(C(q') - C(q)),$$

so $B(q') = 0$. If $B'(q')$ does not equal zero then there must exist some point, q'', arbitrarily close to q' where followers are not consuming, where $B(q'') < 0$, and hence $s(q'') = 1$. Leaders will then deviate to q''. A pooling equilibrium can only exist where $B(q'') > 0$, for all q'' near to q', which requires that $B'(q') = 0$ and $B'(q') > 0$. The quality level $\hat{q}$ is the unique solution to $B'(q) = 0$ and $B''(\hat{q}) > 0$. If either $\alpha < \beta$ or $1 < \beta$ (but not both), then $\hat{q}$ is negative, which means there is no pooling point. If

$\alpha < \beta$ and $1 < \beta$, then $B''(q) < 0$ for all q, so there cannot be a pooling equilibrium.

Part 1 of Proposition 7.1 If $q_L^* > q_F^+$ or $q_F^- > q_L^*$, then a unique stable equilibrium exists where leaders choose q_L^* and followers choose q_F^*.

This equilibrium exists because leaders prefer q_L^* to any other point and followers prefer q_F^* to imitating the leaders at q_L^*. Any deviation between q_F^+ and q_F^- will be taken as coming from followers so there is no incentive for followers to deviate, and any deviation outside of those points will yield lower utility to followers even if the deviation is thought of as coming from a leader.

In a separating equilibrium, from Lemma 1 followers always choose q_F^*. If leaders choose a value other than q_L^*, they could deviate to q_L^* and that deviation would always be thought of as coming from a leader (since the followers could only lose utility through such a deviation). From Lemma 3, a pooling equilibrium can only exist at $\hat{q}$, but at this pooling equilibrium, leaders can always deviate and select q_L^* and that deviation will be thought of as coming from a leader.

Part 2 of Proposition 7.1 When $q_F^+ > q_L^* > q_F^-$, if $\beta > \alpha$, or $\beta > 1$, or $\hat{q} > q_F^+$ or $q_F^- > \hat{q}$, then a unique stable equilibrium exists where followers choose q_F^* and leaders choose q_F^- if $1 > \alpha$ or q_F^+ if $\alpha > 1$.

From Lemma 3, if either $\beta > \alpha$, or $\beta > 1$, then only separating equilibria exist. If $\hat{q} > q_F^+$ or $q_F^- > \hat{q}$, then a pooling equilibrium cannot exist because followers will always prefer q_F^* to $\hat{q}$.

In separating equilibria when $q_F^+ > q_L^* > q_F^-$, followers choose q_F^* (from Lemma 1) and leaders choose q_F^- if $1 > \alpha$ and q_F^+ if $\alpha > 1$ (from Lemma 2). We prove existence in the case where $\alpha > 1$:

$$B(q) = \frac{\alpha - \beta}{\beta}(V(q_F^+) - V(q)) - \frac{1 - \beta}{\beta}(C(q_F^+) - C(q))$$

and $B(q_F^+) = 0$. As long as

$$B'(q_F^+) = \frac{1-\beta}{\beta} C'(q_F^+) - \frac{\alpha - \beta}{\beta} V'(q_F^+) < 0 \quad \text{or}$$

$$(\alpha - \beta) > (1 - \beta) > (1 - \beta)\frac{C'(q_F^+)}{V'(q_F^+)},$$

then $B(q) > 0$ and $s(q) = 0$ for all q less than q_F^+. As $C'(q)/V'(q)$ is rising with q, then this clearly holds when $\hat{q} > q_F^+$. The case where $q_F^- > \hat{q}$ cannot occur when $\alpha > 1$, as that implies that $q_F^* > \hat{q}$, but $V'(q_F^*)$ and $V'(\hat{q}) < C'(\hat{q})$ (when $\alpha > 1$) which implies $\hat{q} > q_F^*$. If $\beta > \alpha > 1$ or $\alpha > \beta > 1$, then the condition becomes:

$$\frac{C'(q_F^+)}{V'(q_F^+)} > \frac{\beta - \alpha}{\beta - 1}.$$

As $C'(q_F^*)/V'(q_F^*) = 1$, and $C'(q)/V'(q)$ is rising with q, this must hold. The case where $\alpha < 1$ is symmetric.

Part 3 of Proposition 7.1 If $\alpha > \beta$, $1 > \beta$ and $q_F^+ > \hat{q} > q_F^-$, then a unique stable equilibrium exists where all leaders and some followers consume $\hat{q}$, and other followers consume q_F^*.

First, we prove existence. As $B(\hat{q}) = 0$, $B'(\hat{q}) = 0$, and $B''(\hat{q}) > 0$, $B(q) > 0$ and $s(q) = 0$ elsewhere, so leaders will not deviate. Followers would only deviate to q_F^*, but utility is equalized between the pooling point and q_F^* for followers so they will not deviate.

Second, we know that no other pooling equilibrium exists by Lemma 3. To prove that a separating equilibrium does not exist, consider a candidate separating equilibrium where followers choose q_F^* and leaders choose q_F^+ (if $\alpha > 1$). Since

$$\frac{1-\beta}{\beta} C'(q_F^+) > \frac{\alpha - \beta}{\beta} V'(q_F^+),$$

$V''(q) < 0$, $C''(q) > 0$, $q_F^+ > \hat{q}$, $\alpha > \beta$, and $1 > \beta$ it follows that

$$\frac{1-\beta}{\beta} C'(q_F^+) > \frac{\alpha - \beta}{\beta} V'(q_F^+),$$

which implies $B'(q_F^+) > 0$. It is also true that $s(q) = 1$ for $q < q_F^+$ and the leaders would deviate downward, since these deviation would be thought to come from them. In the candidate equilibrium where leaders choose q_F^- if $\alpha < 1$, then leaders would deviate upward.

Q.E.D.

CHAPTER 8

Status and Inequality

(with Iván Werning)

1. Introduction

Every known society studied in detail has been found to have considerable inequality in status, where persons with higher "status" receive deference and respect from those with lower status. Since such esteem and respect from others provides pleasure or utility, individuals strive as best they can for higher status. As James Coleman observes (1990, p. 130), "Differential status is universal in social systems . . . status, or recognition from others, has long been regarded by psychologists as a primary source of satisfaction to the self. That is, an interest in status can be regarded as being held by every person."

The previous chapters in this part have ignored the striving for status, and have taken as given the distribution of persons between just two categories of status, high and low. This chapter endogenizes who has higher status by allowing individuals to compete for a limited number of higher-status positions. Successful competitors acquire higher status, while the unsuccessful ones have to accept lower statuses. Instead of assuming only two status categories, we allow possibly many distinct status positions. Indeed, it is analytically more convenient to assume a continuous distribution of status levels instead of a discrete number.

Some forms of status are rigidly fixed, such as that due to caste or ancestors. Others, however, depend on income and wealth; occupation;

education; scientific, political, or business accomplishments; goods consumed; and objects collected. In effect, competition for status means that successful individuals "buy" status, although the currency is not always money. When status comes with scientific accomplishment, status is "purchased" through the efforts and talents that make possible these achievements. If status is given to military heroes, such as winners of the Congressional Medal of Honor, status is "purchased" by the heroism that may also be motivated by patriotism and other considerations.

Although several ways to acquire status are important, we simplify the analysis greatly by concentrating on the competition for higher incomes. Competition for income can represent a more general striving for status, since in every society, individuals and families with greater income and wealth tend to have higher status. Higher income may lead to greater status automatically through the prestige of high ranks in the distribution of income. Or higher income may allow the purchase of goods and objects that bring greater status, including diamonds, art, fancy cars, expensive homes in "good" neighborhoods, greater education, and marriage of children to lords, counts, or other titled persons.

When status can be "purchased," individuals with higher incomes tend to acquire greater status as long as status is a "normal" good. The equilibrium prices of different levels of status are determined in this approach by the forces of supply and demand, as in the usual hedonic analysis (Rosen, 1974).

Although we assume in this chapter a full competitive hedonic market in status, we have shown elsewhere (Becker, Murphy, and Werning, 2000, app.) that this approach is equivalent to the indirect purchase of status through the acquisition of status-producing goods, such as diamonds, art, houses, or education. In the indirect purchase of status, production functions map greater quantities of these goods into the higher-status positions determined by the overall distribution of status.

The many ways to obtain higher incomes include investments in education and other human capital, moves to better-paying localities, accumulation of assets, and so forth. This chapter largely ignores these determinants of the functional distribution of income to concentrate on the demand for risky activities, where winners receive higher incomes and also, directly or indirectly, higher status, while losers get lower incomes and lower status. These risky activities include entrepreneurial efforts, speculation on stocks and options, gambling, lotteries, crime, occupations with uncertain payoffs like law and business administration, and many others.

Our concentration on risky activities does not presuppose that risk taking is a more important determinant of the distribution of income than are investments in human and other types of capital, endowments of abilities and talents, and other determinants of the functional distribution of income. Although risk taking is crucial to our analysis, it extends the functional distribution in order to tailor more carefully the personal distribution of income to a given distribution of status. The functional distribution of income usually explains most of the distribution of personal income even after the effects of risk taking are incorporated.

If the distribution of status and the value placed on higher status are similar in different societies, risk-taking activities make the distributions of personal income also similar, even when the functional income distributions are quite different. Section 4 gives precise conditions for lotteries and other risks to produce the same distribution of income in societies with the same preferences over goods and status, even though they may have quite different functional distributions of income.

In traditional public finance, a utilitarian social planner would reduce inequality by redistributing income from the rich to the poor. In our analysis a social planner, like private markets, tries to match income to status. Given our assumption that consumption and status are complements in utility, a social planner may even redistribute income *from* the poor *to* the rich rather than the other way around. Indeed, section 5 shows that if the functional income inequality is not too large, a utilitarian with access to lump-sum taxes and subsidies would redistribute to the "rich" and create the same distribution of consumption as would private markets that include optimal lotteries.

2. Status and Income

We assume that the utility of each person depends on his or her own consumption and status. This assumption implies that utility does not directly depend on the consumption or status of anyone else. Everyone is assumed to have the same utility function that is rising and concave in own income (equal to consumption, for now); it can be either concave or convex in status:

(8.1) $U = U(I, S)$,   where $U_I > 0$, $U_{II} < 0$,   and $U_S > 0$.

A crucial assumption of the analysis is that a rise in status increases the marginal utility of income or consumption:

(8.2) $U_{IS} > 0$.

Status also affects the marginal utility of leisure, as in Veblen's *Theory of the Leisure Class* (1934; see especially chapter 3). In the interest of simplicity, we ignore the relation between status and leisure.

A positive effect of status on the marginal utility of income is an indication of complementarity between status and income. With complementarity, a rise in status would raise the marginal utility of income, and symmetrically, a rise in income would raise the utility from higher status. This complementarity is crucial to our analysis of the effects of the desire for higher status on income inequality and the propensity to gamble. For although utility is assumed to be concave in income alone, it need not be concave in both income and status if they rise and fall together. That is, higher income could be associated with an increase rather than a decrease in the marginal utility of income if status rises with income.

The analysis in this book considers the complementarity between social forces and various kinds of behavior, including smoking and purchasing jewelry and expensive watches. A natural extension is to complementarity between status—a particular form of social capital—and total consumption itself. One reason for such complementarity is that higher-status persons may have access to consumer goods in limited supply, such as boxes at concerts, desirable neighborhoods, and prestigious clubs that are not available to others, but raise the marginal utility of income to these persons. Moreover, the marginal utility from income may be greater to persons with higher status because the general population expects them to have larger homes with better views, to be more educated and knowledgeable, be leaders in fashion, collect art and other objects, entertain well, travel extensively, and so forth.

A positive cross derivative between status and consumption can also be empirically motivated by the positive relation between status, income, and consumption observed in essentially all known societies. One might have expected the opposite, that higher status would require compensating differentials, or lower income and consumption.

The concept of noncompeting groups was introduced in the nineteenth century partly to explain why status, income, and consumption are positively rather than negatively related. This implies that the competition for status is restricted and limited. Although some groups may be noncompetitive, our analysis will show that noncompeting groups are not needed to explain why higher-income people tend also to have higher status. Although everyone may be identical in our analysis and compete fully, status, income, and consumption will be positively related as long as status and consumption are complements in the utility function.

A second major assumption of our analysis is that the distribution of status categories is given—say it ranges from S_l to S_h. Each of N persons occupies one and only one of these categories, and by equation (8.1), everyone prefers the higher categories. It is analytically more convenient to treat the distribution of status as a continuum, with a frequency distribution $F(S)$. The distribution of status would be uniform between zero and one if status rose with income rank.

It is not unreasonable to assume that the distribution of all determinants of status is fixed and given, at least in the short run. A fixed distribution of status implies that although a person's utility only depends directly on his own status, indirectly it depends on that of others. The availability of these categories to everyone else is reduced when other persons occupy high-status categories. Presumably, status is in more fixed supply relative to most goods—as in status due to higher rank in the income distribution. Otherwise, status would simply be another good in the utility function, and there would be little point in distinguishing status and "goods."

Elsewhere (Becker, Murphy, and Werning, 2000) we show that the assumption of a given distribution of status is equivalent to assuming that status increases with the quantity consumed of a status-producing good, such as diamonds. The market for status is more efficient when the aggregate quantity of this good is relatively fixed, as with diamonds.

3. Buying Status

Even when status does not automatically rise with income, it tends to be positively related to income because the willingness to pay for higher status rises with income. To show how the willingness to pay enters, suppose there is a market to buy status, and that hedonic supply and demand functions produce an equilibrium price function for status, $P(S)$, with $P' > 0$. The cost of status rises with status.

Income can be spent on status as well as on other goods, so consumption and income are not identical. The utility function still depends on consumption and status, but the budget constraint is:

$$(8.3) \qquad\qquad C + P(S) = I.$$

If utility is maximized subject to this constraint, the FOC for everyone is

$$(8.4) \qquad\qquad \frac{U_S}{U_C} = P'(S).$$

In equation (8.4), everyone adjusts his consumption and status to the market price function $P(S)$ and her own income. If status is a superior good, it rises with income. In particular, if utility is quasi-concave in C and S, and if $U_{CC} < 0$ and $U_{CS} > 0$ by equation (8.2), then equation (8.4) implies that

$$(8.5) \qquad \frac{dS^*}{dI} = \frac{U_{CC}P' - U_{SC}}{D} > 0, \quad \text{because } D < 0 \text{ by the SOC.}$$

Equation (8.5) implies a positive relation between status and income: $S^* = H(I)$, with $H' > 0$. The distribution of S^* must equal the exogenous distribution of status mediated by the cumulative distribution of income. It follows from this function and from equation (8.5) that

$$(8.6) \qquad\qquad P'(S^*) = \frac{U_s\{C(I), H(I)\}}{U_c\{C(I), H(I)\}}.$$

This equation determines P', given the utility function, the distribution of income, and the equilibrium function $S^* = H(I)$. The revenue from the sale of status is given by the integral of $P(S^*)$ over the distribution of status. This revenue has little effect on the analysis if it is distributed equally to everyone (see the appendix to this chapter).

As equation (8.5) indicates, higher income raises the demand for greater status, perhaps in the form of higher education; more prestigious occupations; property in better neighborhoods; the "buying" of diamonds, art, and of titles and church privileges; and many other ways. This does not mean that Nobel Prizes and the like are for sale, but only that often a person raises the likelihood, not the certainty, of attaining various kinds of higher status by spending more effort and money on acquiring status. Moreover, while the price function $P(S)$ deals with the extreme case of complete markets in status, where any level of status can be purchased if a person is willing to pay its market price, much of our analysis is applicable with less extreme assumptions.

If lotteries determine the equilibrium distribution of consumption and the covariance of consumption with status, the equilibrium distribution of income would be determined by both the equilibrium distribution of consumption and the price of status. That is, aside from the distribution of proceeds from the sale of status, income is determined by equation (8.3), where I, C, and P depend on S^*. Since $P(S^*)$ rises with S^* and C, income is more unequally distributed than consumption.

Economic development increases income, but presumably development has a much smaller, if any, effect on the supply of status. For example, the distribution of income ranks is independent of average income level, and it is not obvious whether other forms of prestige and status are in significantly greater supply now than at the at the end of the nineteenth century, or several centuries ago.

If status becomes relatively scarcer as economies develop, the price of status would rise relative to that of consumption goods. Clearly, the willingness to pay for a fixed amount of status, given by equation (8.4), would rise as average incomes grew since the marginal utility of goods, U_C, would fall, and the marginal utility of given status, U_S, would increase. The increase in U_S would be especially large when status and consumption are complements. Moreover, with diminishing marginal utility of consumption, a fixed supply of status would become an increasing drag on utilities as consumption grew over time.

4. The Private Distribution of Income

Complementarity between consumption and status implies that individuals with greater consumption and status may have higher marginal utility of consumption than those with lower status and lower consumption. In that case, both richer and poorer individuals would be willing to take fair gambles, through lotteries or other risky activities, in which winners get *both* higher consumption and higher status, and losers get lower consumption and lower status. The result would be a possibly highly unequal distribution of consumption and utility, with status and consumption positively related.

Although the analysis applies to any number of individuals and status categories, we can illustrate the principles involved graphically with two individuals A and B, who have the same utility function, and two status categories, S_0 and $S_1 > S_0$. Figure 8.1 plots the relation between income and utility for each of these categories. The curve labeled S_0 assumes a person has the lower status at all income levels. This curve is concave because of the assumption that utility is concave in consumption and income for a given status level.

This figure also plots the utility-income relation for someone with S_1. This curve is also concave throughout, but it is below the S_0 curve for incomes less than I_c. We assume following the discussion in section 3 that it is costly to acquire S_1, so that utility with S_1 would be below utility with S_0 for incomes below, say, I_c, and it would be above the utility with S_0 only for higher incomes (above I_c). The person with income I_c

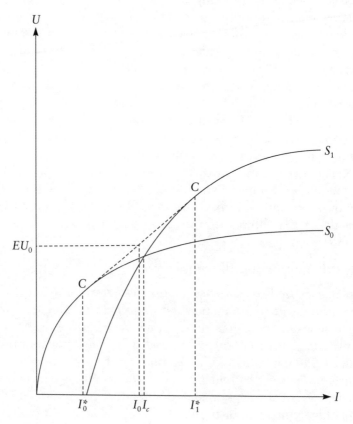

Figure 8.1

and status S_0 would have the same utility as the person with income I_c and the higher-status S_1 because the consumption of the latter would be sufficiently lower to compensate fully for her higher status.

For two reasons the slope of the S_1 curve exceeds the slope of the S_0 curve at I_c. Consumption is lower at I_c with S_1, and the marginal utility of consumption is decreasing. Moreover, the positive cross derivative between C and S means that the marginal utility of consumption would be higher with S_1 even if consumptions were the same. The higher slope of the S_1 curve implies that the frontier or envelope between the two curves is convex in a region because of the cusp at the intersection point I_c (see also Friedman, 1953; Rosen, 1997).

This convexity implies that if A and B each initially have income I_0, they will be willing to participate in fair lotteries, where the winner gets *both* higher income and higher status. The optimal fair lottery would be determined by the chord CC that is tangent to the envelope at the two points I_0^* and I_1^*. The expected utility of A and B equals EU_0, which is much above their utility without the lottery. In this optimal lottery, the winner gets both a much higher income, I_1^*, and the higher status, S_1.

The tangency condition for the optimal lottery implies that it equalizes the marginal utility of consumption to both winners and losers, as in:

$$(8.7) \qquad U_c(C_1^*, S_1) = U_c(C_0^*, S_0).$$

Equal marginal utilities of consumption is a general condition that applies with N individuals who participate in a fair lottery with N status categories and N consumption outcomes. It also applies with continuous distributions of status and individuals. Given complementarity between consumption and status, persons who win higher status also win greater consumption. It may be necessary to pay more for higher status, but then income would be sufficiently high so that consumption would be greater net of the cost of status—see section 3.

In effect, there is a lottery in both consumption and status since winners get both higher incomes and higher status—although they must pay for higher status. The lottery in status is essential, since there would not be a demand for lotteries without the inequality in status given that utility is assumed to be concave in consumption alone.

Both A and B will participate in fair lotteries as long as their incomes are between I_0^* and I_1^*. Even if utility is separable in C and S, they will still gain from fair lotteries if their incomes are in this interval. However, in the separable case, equal marginal utilities of consumption imply equal consumptions, so that the lottery offers a gamble only in status and utility, and "insures" consumption. With complementarity between consumption and status, winners of these lotteries get higher consumption and higher status, and of course higher utility.

This demonstrates that complementarity is necessary to explain the observed positive relation between consumption and status among competing individuals. Without gambles, there would be a compensating differential for higher status, so that persons with higher status would have lower consumption and the same utility as others. Even separability between consumption and status can induce lotteries where winners get higher status and higher utility, but they do not get higher consumption. Only if consumption and status are complements will winners get higher status *and* higher consumption, which is the empirically important case.

These results are illuminated further by Figure 8.2, where the utility of A is plotted along the horizontal axis, and that of B is plotted along the vertical axis. If B had the higher status, the utility possibility boundary would be given by the negatively sloped concave curve BB as income is reallocated between A and B. Similarly, the boundary would be the concave curve AA if A had the higher status. The slope of these boundaries at each point equals the marginal utility of consumption to A relative to that of B, given the distribution of status between A and B.

The economy's boundary is the symmetrical curve BEA that is the envelope of the two curves AA and BB. This boundary has a kink at point E, and the assumption of equal utility functions means that E must lie on the 45-degree line. The economy's boundary is not everywhere concave—the utility possibility set is not everywhere convex—because there is a shift at point E of higher status from A to B as income and status are redistributed from A to B. The assumed complementarity between status and consumption raises the marginal utility of consumption to B and lowers it to A by discrete amounts when B's status is increased.

The incentives to engage in lotteries can be shown by using this kinked utility-possibility frontier. With actuarially fair lotteries, winners get higher utility, consumption, and status, and the marginal utility of consumption is the same to winners and losers—as in equation (8.7). The marginal utility of consumption is the same to A and B at the two

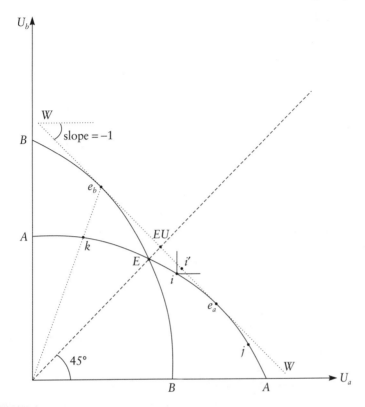

Figure 8.2

symmetrical points e_b and e_a in Figure 8.2, where the slope of the utility frontier equals -1. Then the expected utility of both A and B would lie along the chord WW with a slope of -1 that is tangent to these points.

If the initial position of A and B is on BEA between points e_b and e_a, both A and B would participate in fair lotteries. If they have the same initial income and utility at point E, they would have equal chances of winning the lottery, and their expected utility position would be on WW at point EU along the 45-degree line.

If initially utility is higher to A than to B at point i, the expected utility position would be on WW to the right and above point i, say at i'. Although A gets the same consumption and status as B both when they win and when they lose, A has the higher probability of winning C_1 and S_1 because A starts with high income: $I_A > I_B$. As I_A increases relative to I_B, the difference between their probabilities of winning also increases.

The extreme is reached when $I_A = I_1^*$, and $I_B = I_0^*$, for then A is certain to win and B is certain to lose. It is clear from Figure 8.2 that neither A nor B would be interested in fair lotteries if A's income were sufficiently large to push the initial position to the right of e_a. A symmetrical analysis applies to B.

The optimal fair lottery increases the ex-post inequality in utility, consumption, and income as long as initial incomes are between I_0^* and I_1^*. Moreover, the equilibrium distribution of income, consumption, and utility is unique, *regardless* of the initial position, as long as the initial utility position is between e_a and e_b in Figure 8.2. Put differently, there is a unique distribution of utility, consumption, and income as long as the marginal utility of consumption is initially higher to the person who initially has higher status. To use Rosen's felicitous language (1997), an economy "manufactures" a unique degree of inequality through the desires of individuals to participate in lotteries in income and consumption.

This analysis fully generalizes to a continuum of individuals and status categories. If all individuals are identical, they all participate in fair lotteries that would equalize the marginal utility of consumption to persons at all status positions (for a proof, see section A.2 of the appendix). With complementarity between consumption and status, equal marginal utilities of consumption imply that persons who win the highest status also win the highest consumption and highest income, and persons who get the lowest status also get the lowest consumption and lowest income.

To generalize the formal analysis to a continuum of statuses and incomes, let Y^* be the equilibrium distribution of income when everyone is identical. Let Y^o be the initial distribution of income determined by human capital and other functional attributes. Assume that Y^* is obtained from Y^o by a mean-preserving increase in spread, as in

(8.8) $$Y^* = Y^o + e,$$

where $E(e \mid Y^o) = 0$. Then optimal fair lotteries convert the Y^o distribution into the equilibrium distribution Y^*, where the distribution of e gives the outcomes from this lottery (see Becker, Murphy, Werning, 2000, for a proof).

Equation (8.8) generalizes the analysis for two persons in Figures 8.1 and 8.2. The requirement that Y^* and Y^o be related by a mean-preserving increase in spread is the analytical meaning of the statement that there is an equilibrium distribution of income when the initial income distribution is sufficiently compact. The optimal lottery widens the distribution of income in order to better match income and consumption to status; that is, in order to equalize the marginal utility of consumption at different status levels.

Actual income distributions usually have considerable inequality and right-side skewness. The inequality and skewness in the equilibrium distribution Y^* clearly depend on the inequality and skewness in the distribution of status, since consumption is matched to status. Although the hierarchy implied by the distribution of status appears to be quite skewed as well as unequal, no one has developed natural units by which to measure status.

Therefore, to avoid "assuming" the shape of the equilibrium distribution of income, we assume that status has a symmetrical distribution. Perhaps status has a uniform distribution, as when status depends on income rank. Then the inequality and skewness in income would crucially depend on preferences over status and consumption. Equality of the marginal utilities of consumption at all status levels implies that the elasticity of consumption with respect to status equals the elasticity of the marginal utility of consumption with respect to status divided by the absolute value of the elasticity of the marginal utility of consumption with respect to consumption.

If status is symmetrically distributed, equilibrium consumption will be more unequally distributed than status, and consumption will be skewed to the right only if the ratio of these consumption elasticities exceeds one. Consumption will be less unequally distributed than status and it will be skewed to the left if the ratio of these elasticities is below one. If the utility function is homothetic, then the ratio of these elasticities equals one, exceeds one, or is below one, as the utility function has constant, increasing, or decreasing returns in consumption and status.

"Lotteries" should be interpreted quite generally to include all kinds of risky activities in the real sector, including entrepreneurial ventures through startups; efforts to discover new goods, processes, and medical treatments; other risky investments; and even criminal activities. Sections 6 and 7 briefly discuss various implications of this more general interpretation of the risky choices involved in lotteries.

Our emphasis on the effect of lotteries and other gambles on the equilibrium distribution of income and consumption does not minimize the importance of wage differentials due to differences in skills; unionization; abilities; race, gender, and other personal characteristics; differences in inherited wealth and savings; and other aspects of the *functional* distribution of income. The functional distribution determines the important initial income distribution that determines both whether equation (8.8) is satisfied and the probabilities to different persons of doing well in the lottery.

If the functional distribution of income satisfies equation (8.8), everyone will participate in a fair lottery that equalizes all marginal utilities of consumption. People with higher functional incomes receive correspondingly higher expected incomes in a fair lottery, so that they have higher probabilities of winning the better statuses and higher incomes. Nevertheless, the optimal distributions of income, consumption, status, and utility are completely independent of the functional distribution of income, as long as that distribution satisfies equation (8.8).

No one would be willing to participate in fair lotteries if the status of each individual were fully and irrevocably determined by family background, personal achievements, and other considerations. For then each person's status would be fixed and no one would accept fair lotteries, because the marginal utility of income would be diminishing for a given status level. In this case, the utility possibility curve would be everywhere concave; in Figure 8.2, it would be given by either *BB* or *AA*. But not all forms of status are completely fixed. Indeed, it would defeat the social purpose of unequal statuses if individuals could not strive to improve at least some dimensions of their status.

5. "Socially Optimal" Income Inequality

This section considers the "optimal" distribution of income by a planner who maximizes a social welfare function. We mainly consider a utilitarian who maximizes the sum of utilities, although we briefly consider other criteria as well. Our purpose is to show that the importance of status can radically change the optimal income distribution implied by utilitarian and other social welfare functions. Indeed, they may imply greater income inequality than the inequality produced by market outcomes.

The analytical motivation for the assumption in optimal tax theory that taxes and subsidies distort behavior is to help explain why the optimal income distribution to a utilitarian might still have considerable inequality. There is no need in our discussion to assume distorting taxes and subsidies, since the status distribution implies considerable consumption and income inequality even with lump-sum redistributions.

In the conventional problem without status, a utilitarian faced with diminishing marginal utility of incomes, and using lump-sum taxes and subsidies, would redistribute sufficient income from rich to poor to equalize everyone's marginal utility of income. If everyone has the same utility function, this implies equal consumptions, incomes, and utilities as well.

We assume that everyone has the same utility functions that depend on status as well as on consumption. If a utilitarian could arbitrarily assign status as well as income, he would allocate incomes and statuses to individuals to equalize the marginal utilities of consumption to everyone, as in equation (8.7) (see section A.1 of the appendix).

The assumption of complementarity between status and income implies that the social planner would assign higher status rather than lower status to persons who receive higher incomes and higher consumptions. The utilitarian's optimum can be shown in Figure 8.2 with two individuals, A and B. WW can be interpreted as an indifference curve of the utilitarian welfare function, for these curves have a slope equal to -1. A utilitarian maximizes social welfare by going to the points of tangency of an indifference curve with the utility-possibility frontier. In this case, there are two symmetrical tangency points at e_a and e_b, where A has the higher status and higher consumption at e_a, and B has the correspondingly higher status and higher consumption at e_b.

These tangency points have the same marginal utility of consumption to the persons who receive high or low status. It is rather remarkable that these are also the equilibrium distributions of consumption and status produced by market lotteries when the initial "functional" utility position is between e_a and e_b. In other words, the ex-post distributions of income and status in this case produced by a utilitarian are exactly the same as those produced by selfish market participants.

In the usual analysis there is a major conflict between the income distribution proposed by a utilitarian planner and that produced by private choices, because it is usually assumed that the marginal utility of consumption is lower to individuals with higher incomes. This is plausible if utility only depends on income, and if individuals are assumed to have the same utility functions. In that case, equation (8.7) is still the first-order condition for a utilitarian who would redistribute income from richer to poorer persons. Individuals do not accept fair lotteries in this case because greater uncertainty lowers the expected utility of both high- and low-income individuals.

We have seen, however, that the conclusion will be radically different if utility also depends on status, and if consumption and status are complements. Then the utilitarian and the market may arrive at the same distribution of income and status, as in Figure 8.2.

A utilitarian has no way of choosing between e_a and e_b and, like the market, might randomize the outcome through lotteries. The expected utilities of A and B would lie along the indifference curve WW joining e_b and e_a. Since each person has equal weight to a utilitarian, the expected utilities of A and B are on the 45-degree line at point EU on WW.

Although the expected utilities EU are equal, the actual utilities of A and B at either e_a or e_b would involve sizable inequality. If the initial position prior to redistribution was between e_a and e_b, say at point i on the boundary, a utilitarian would reduce the inequality in expected utilities but would significantly raise the inequality in realized consumptions, incomes, and utilities.

Of course, other social welfare functions would give different results, but they all are radically affected by recognizing the importance of status. For example, would a Rawlsian equalize expected utilities in status and consumption, at point EU—which is the same position chosen by a utilitarian—or actual utilities, at point E, by offering the person with lower status a sufficiently large compensating increase in income?

While point EU is implementable, participants would try to undo any attempt by a Rawlsian to implement E. Starting from E, they would participate in fair lotteries that would bring their expected utilities to EU, and their actual utilities to considerable inequality at either e_a or e_b. Given the choice philosophy behind the veil of ignorance approach, a Rawlsian presumably would not want to prevent these lotteries and their potential enormous effects on inequality in consumption, status, income, and utility.

A utilitarian or a Rawlsian would tend to have less inequality in *expected* utility than the market does, even when they have the same ex-post inequality. Initial conditions determined by the functional distribution of income do not matter to such planners who can use lump-sum redistributions, but they greatly matter to market participants. Regardless of initial conditions—for example, whether at points E, i, or j in Figure 8.2—the utilitarian equalizes expected utility at point EU, whereas the market goes from i to expected utilities at i', and individuals at j would refuse fair lotteries. Of course, initial conditions become more important the greater the deadweight cost of redistributing incomes, but a social planner still gives less weight to these conditions than the market does.

Yet sometimes the status distribution would induce a utilitarian to raise the inequality in utility and consumption compared to market outcomes. The utility-possibility boundary BEA in Figure 8.2 assumes that either A or B could have higher status, which helps produce the symmetry in this boundary. If A came from an eminent family, or for other reasons necessarily had the higher status, the boundary would be given by AA. This boundary is fully concave and not symmetrical between A and B, even though they have the same utility functions. Social welfare to a utilitarian is then maximized at point e_a on this boundary.

Since e_a is one of the equilibrium points when either A or B could have the higher status, the optimal ex-post inequality to a utilitarian does not depend on whether he can assign status, or whether instead status is tied to individuals. The ex-post equilibrium distribution of utility, consumption, and income is exactly the same in both cases. When status is tied, however, a utilitarian will not randomize, because point e_b in Figure 8.2 is not attainable.

When status is tied to individuals, markets do not create lotteries because all participants have diminishing marginal utility of consumption for their given fixed status. Therefore, whether markets or a utilitarian produces greater inequality in income, consumption, and utility when status is tied to the individual depends on the degree of inequality in the functional distribution of utility.

6. Entrepreneurial and Risky Investments versus Lotteries

Our analysis implies that lotteries would be important if given the functional distribution of income, the marginal utility of income were higher to persons with greater incomes and status because of the complementarity between status and income. Yet although actual lotteries are popular and highly profitable to government monopolies, only lower-income families typically spend more than a small fraction of their income on lottery tickets.

Some persons have concluded from the unimportance of lotteries that most persons are risk averse, and that they are reluctant to gamble more than a small fraction of their wealth. However, before also inferring from this evidence that status is neither important nor complementary with income, consider an alternative explanation for the unimportance of lotteries.

Suppose that many, perhaps most, higher-income persons can gamble through equities, occupational choices, and entrepreneurial activities. Lotteries would be of little value to them because they have superior ways to gamble through utilizing the productive risks in an economy. Even an actuarially fair lottery has only a zero expected return, and most government lotteries are far from "fair" since they impose a heavy tax on lottery tickets. By contrast, stocks and bonds usually yield a positive expected return, and although entrepreneurial activities are even riskier, the returns can be very high.

Therefore, a desire to gamble may be more productively satisfied through the positive-sum gambles provided by human, physical, and financial capital investments than through negative-sum or even zero-sum lotteries (see the discussion of entrepreneurial activities and lotteries in Brenner, 1983). We believe this explains why startups and other entrepreneurial efforts, attempts to find new goods, better production processes, and medical treatments, and other risky activities are much more common than would be expected from the usual assumptions of risk aversion and diminishing marginal utility of income.

Crime is sometimes also an alternative to lotteries since criminal activities are risky and can be very profitable. Apparently criminals tend to be risk preferrers, since they are more affected by changes in the probability of apprehension and conviction than by equal percentage changes in the size of punishments (see the proof in Becker, 1968). Drug dealing and other crimes may be attractive to ghetto and other poor young people because these are their best, though highly risky, route to higher status as well as higher incomes. The demand for higher status along with higher income also explains why stock manipulation and other white-collar crimes have been attractive to many members of the middle class.

7. Status, Rank, and Efficiency

It has been argued that a fixed distribution of status leads to excessive competition for status, because higher status for some people necessarily implies lower status and utility for others. This point of view has been most eloquently advanced by Robert Frank (1999), but also see, among others, Robson (1992) and Cole, Mailath, and Postlewaite (1992). Frank has one chapter entitled "Smart for One, Dumb for All," and even claims (p. 159) that "when each family saves less to buy a house in a better school district, the net effect is *merely* to bid up the prices of those houses . . . In the process . . . being able to maintain an adequate living standard . . . is sacrificed for essentially no gain" (emphasis added). He makes numerous related claims in this and earlier books.

Competition for status is sometimes excessive, but much of this competition is consistent with efficiency. For example, we have shown that competition for status is fully consistent with efficiency when status can be purchased in a competitive marketplace, like Frank's "house in a better school district." Then the cost of acquiring higher status is simply a transfer payment that adds to the sellers' wealth, and the market value of houses is also an asset for buyers.

The same conclusion applies to competition in marriage and related markets, where individuals who improve their attractiveness ipso facto lower the *relative* attractiveness of their competitors. We show in Chapter 4 that competition for mates is fully efficient if the value someone brings to a marriage, or other matches, is fully priced. A nice application of that analysis is to Frank's discussion of wearing high heels, a seemingly plausible example of excessive competition: "The height advantage someone gains by wearing high-heeled shoes is neutralized once high heel shoes become the norm" (1999, p. 158). Yet the demand for high heels is efficient, even when such shoes cause foot and back damage, if the marriage, or other, markets that match men and women compensate women fully for the utility gain to their husbands or other companions from their wearing high heels. This behavior is efficient even when it lowers the relative attractiveness of other women, including women who also wear high heels.

Women who are aware of the damage caused by wearing high heels would factor that into their decisions. They would have to trade off any damage for the greater utility from getting better spouses and other companions. Indeed, there will be too *little* wearing of high heels from an efficiency perspective if women's wearing high heels gives pleasure to other men when they walk, and if these "bystanders" do not compensate the women for the utility they receive.

To be sure, we also show in Chapter 4 that investments in human capital and other personal advantages, like high heels, may be excessive if marriage and other matching markets do not price contributions according to marginal products. Yet we show there that the absence of effective pricing can also discourage socially optimal investments in various forms of human capital. Strong, and often unreasonable, assumptions about the role of marital and other pricing lie behind criticisms by Frank and others of the competition for better matches.

A person's marginal utility of income often rises when the income of a peer rises—such as that of a fellow employee, neighbor, or friend. But that simply implies that the *cross* derivative of utility is positive with respect to own income and their incomes. It does not imply that the sign of the *first* derivative of utility with respect to their incomes is negative, a common assumption in the analysis by Frank and other critics of competition for higher incomes.

Indeed, utility clearly often increases rather than decreases when individuals have contact with other persons who have higher incomes than their own. People frequently prefer richer rather than poorer friends, neighbors, and classmates. They pay for the right to drive through the Seventeen-Mile Drive near Monterey, California, and other elite neighborhoods to see how the very wealthy live, and they are eager to hear gossip about the lives of the rich and famous. If higher incomes of others bothered people so much, they would seek poorer peers (as in Frank, 1985), avoid gossip about the lives of the rich, and require compensation rather than paying to see the homes and living conditions of the rich.

Competition for status might even raise efficiency compared with the situation when utility does not depend on status. If the marginal utility of income is diminishing, and if status were unimportant, people would dislike entrepreneurship, R&D investments, and other highly risky activities. They would require extra compensation to engage in these activities if they were risk averse. Some economists have suggested government subsidies for such highly risky activities because of "underinvestment" in these activities due to the alleged importance of risk aversion (see Arrow and Lind, 1970).

Any "underinvestment" in risky activities like entrepreneurship and R&D will then be greater if they confer positive benefits on others through new inventions and the like. Status and its complementarity with consumption could contribute significantly to raising efficiency by encouraging investments in positive-sum risky ventures that may also have sizable positive externalities. Great scientists and outstanding entrepreneurs receive enormous prestige and status precisely in order to encourage scientific and startup activities.

Our discussion does not deny that some forms of competition for status may lower rather than raise efficiency. For example, a person may work long hours mainly to raise his relative income, and hence status, above that of others. If everyone worked equally long and hard, no one's rank and status would change in equilibrium because all incomes would increase proportionately. However, the utility of everyone could go down because all worked "excessively."

These "rat race" examples have received a significant amount of attention (see Cole, Mailath, and Postlewaite, 1992; Frank, 1999), but we believe they are less important than the many situations where competition for status offsets the tendency toward underinvestment in entrepreneurship and other risky activities. To put this differently, critics stress the "rat race" aspects of the competition for status, whereas we believe in the American dream that competition to "get ahead" makes a society function better, not worse.

This conclusion receives "evolutionary" support from the evidence that status is distributed unequally in essentially every society that has been studied, regardless of culture or stage of economic development. Moreover, status usually tends to rise with income, although status is also determined by other characteristics.

Societies that reward higher incomes and other achievements with greater status may have been partially selected by social evolution, because that helps motivate people to engage in risky activities that have beneficial effects on others. The alternative story, that competition for status is a "rat race" drag on efficiency, is hard to reconcile with the general importance of this competition. The attempt to improve one's status also encourages crimes and other risky activities that harm others, but still the competition for status is likely on balance to have contributed to improved outcomes.

Appendix 8A: Lottery Allocation

In what follows we treat with greater detail the allocation for the case where all agents are identical and have identical income levels.

A.1. The Planner's Problem

The planner solves the following problem,

$$\max_{c(s)} \int u[c(s),\, s]g(s)ds$$

$$\int c(s)g(s)ds = \bar{y}.$$

This can be interpreted in either of two extreme ways: (1) the planner is a utilitarian (either controlling or taking as given the assignments of s; it does not matter) and in choosing $c(s)$ he is choosing the consumption for each agent who is treated differently in equilibrium; (2) the planner is maximizing the ex-ante welfare of a lottery over social statuses, and in this case the planner is treating everyone equally, assigning the same ex-ante utility level. Of course intermediate interpretations are also valid, where a lottery is played, with some agents favored over others in their chances.

The FOC of this problem is

$$(8A.1) \qquad\qquad u_c[c(s), s] = \lambda_p,$$

where λ_p is the planner's multiplier on the economy-wide constraint.

A.2. The Private Lotteries Equilibrium

Now agents can consume c and s: they must purchase s at price $P(s)$ with income y. For a given income level they then solve

$$v(y) \equiv \max_{c,s} u(c, s)$$

$$c + P(s) = y.$$

We shall assume the necessary assumptions so that the solution $s^*(y)$ is increasing in $y : s'(y) > 0$.

They can play ex ante a fair lottery over income with the rest of the agents. Therefore, they solve

$$\max_{f(y)} \int v(y) f(y) dy$$

$$\int f(y) = 1$$

$$\int y f(y) dy = \bar{y} + \int P(s) g(s) ds.$$

Here $\bar{y}$ represents the wage income and $\int P(s)g(s)ds$ the income from the equally shared status endowment. The FOC for this problem implies that for all income levels where $f(y) > 0$ we have

$$v(y) = \lambda_m y + \mu,$$

where λ_m is the agent's Lagrange multiplier on income. Using the envelope condition, we have that $v'(y) = u_c(c^*(y), s^*(y))$. Differentiating the above expression we then get

(8A.2) $$u_c[c(y), s(y)] = \lambda_m.$$

The planner's solution and the private solution must coincide. Equations (8A.1) and (8A.2) in equilibrium will actually be the same, since we shall prove that $\lambda_m = \lambda_p$. First we define an equilibrium formally. To simplify the definition we treat the case where in equilibrium s and y are positively related.

Definition A positively sorted competitive-lottery equilibrium is a price function, $P(s)$, a lottery density $f(y)$ and consumption and status conditional demands $c(y)$ and $s(y)$, increasing in y, such that

1. Given $P(s)$, $f(y)$ solves the consumer's lottery problem; given y, the demands $c(y)$ and $s(y)$ solve the consumer's consumption problem.
2. Markets clear:
   1. A fraction $f(y)$ of agents are assigned income y.
   2. The consumption market clears: $\int c(y)f(y)dy = \bar{y}$.
   3. The status market clears: $f(y) = g(s(y))s'(y)$ for all y.

Remark 1 We can always redefine preferences over s so that $g(s) = 1$ and s belongs to the set $S = [0, 1]$. In this case we would have in equilibrium: $f(y) = s'(y)$ for all y.

Remark 2 Notice that the clearing of the goods market is implied given market clearing in all other markets, a Walras's law for our economy. Integrating the consumer's conditional budget constraint over y yields

$$\int c(y)f(y)dy + \int P(s)f(y)dy = \int yf(y)dy$$

Now we know that the fraction of agents obtaining a given $s(y)$ or less is equal to

$$G(s(y)) = F(y),$$

since $s(y)$ is increasing in y. Therefore,

$$g(s(y))s'(y) = f(y),$$

implying that $f(y)dy = g(s)ds$. We also have that $\int yf(y)dy = \bar{y} + \int P(s)g(s)ds$ so we obtain that any equilibrium is satisfying

(8A.3) $$\int c(y)f(y)dy = \bar{y}.$$

We now show that the market equilibrium yields the same joint distribution over c and s:

Proposition 8.1   The equilibrium and the planner's outcome imply the same distribution of c and s.

To see this notice that in equilibrium $s^*(y)$ and $c^*(y)$ define relationships between (c, s) and y. We can relate c and s as follows. Define the function $c^e(s) = c^*(s^{*-1}(s))$. It follows that

$$\int c^e(s)g(s)ds = \bar{y}$$

In equilibrium we also have

$$u_c(c^e(s), s) = \lambda_m$$

for all s. These last two equations are identical to the two equations the planner solves. Therefore it must be true that $\lambda_m = \lambda_p$ and $c^e(s) = c(s)$.

As a working assumption we are assuming that agents choose the same $f(y)$ in equilibrium. It is obvious that this is not necessarily the case. In the equilibrium we have described, agents will actually be indifferent between playing the lottery or not playing the lottery because the price function $P(s)$ adjusts until agents are risk neutral over income. This is due to our assumption of a continuum of social status.

Because we have a continuum of agents, it is not necessary for all of them to participate in the lottery to implement the equilibrium allocation. As long as only a countable set of agents do not participate, the same allocation can be implemented. Furthermore, those who participate could take different lotteries with the average lottery between them looking like the one we singled out.

We know that the planner and the private lottery-equilibria yield the same consumption-status distribution. We can use this to compute prices, $P(s)$. In equilibrium we know that

$$\frac{u_s(c(s), s)}{u_c(c(s), s)} = P'(s).$$

We can therefore solve $P(s)$ as

$$P(s) = \int_{\underline{s}}^{s} \frac{u_s(c(s), s)}{u_c(c(s), s)} ds + P(\underline{s})$$

This determines the function up to a constant. We cannot determine the value of $P(\underline{s})$; any value will achieve the equilibrium.

Fads, Fashions, and Norms

CHAPTER 9

Fads and Fashion

1. Introduction

Fads and fashions include hoola hoops, carrot-tofu birthday cakes, personal nutritionists, words like "obscene" and "camp," windsurfing, the length of women's skirts, deconstructionism, and other goods, activities, and views that rather suddenly become highly popular and then often sharply decline in popularity. Although both fads and fashion crucially depend on popularity, fashions are usually set by elites and other leaders and then copied by followers, whereas fads generally develop more spontaneously. They sometimes even start among the most unlikely of groups, such as teenagers or poor ghetto residents.

The analysis in Part I can be used to show how social considerations determine the rise and fall of fads. That part demonstrated that popular activities do have interesting dynamics because a rise or fall in popularity encourages further changes in the same direction. Increased demand for an activity raises its popularity directly, and also indirectly by increasing demands of others. This dynamic process can create rapid increases and decreases in demand.

The desire of followers to emulate leaders, considered in Part II, along with the wishes of leaders to be separated from followers, also have unusual dynamics. Leaders may initiate a style of clothing or decoration that is later adopted by their followers. At that point, leaders may decide to change their styles in order to distinguish themselves anew from their imitators.

Section 2 formalizes dynamic changes in fads; section 3 examines some dynamics of fashions.

2. Fads

Both the sudden rise and sudden fall of fads suggests that they have a built-in instability, that even small negative shocks to a faddish activity may induce cumulative falls in demand that would kill the fad. Goods and activities demanded in part because they are popular with others can produce such instabilities because changes in popularity induce further cumulative changes in the same direction. Therefore, the stronger the influence of popularity, the larger are the possible destabilizing rises and falls in demand due to even minor shocks.

To show the link between popularity and cumulative changes, follow the discussion in Chapter 2 and write the aggregate demand for a good or activity as

(9.1) $$Q = D(p, Z, Q), \quad \text{with } D_p < 0 \quad \text{and} \quad D_Q > 0,$$

where p is price, Q is the aggregate quantity demanded, and Z are other determinants of demand. The first of the derivatives indicates that demand is still negatively related to price when other factors are the same.

The second of the derivatives incorporates the assumption that demand is raised when it becomes more popular. This means that if the quantity demanded increases, perhaps because of a decline in price, demand will increase still further because the good has become more popular. The result could be large and even unstable responses to quite small shocks. As shown in Chapter 2, the total response to a change in any common variable X, like price, is given by

(9.2) $$\frac{dQ}{dX} = \frac{D_X}{1 - m},$$

where $m = D_Q$ is the social multiplier.

This equation shows that the response to common shocks and other common changes is larger, the stronger the effect of popularity—the larger the social multiplier. A particularly interesting case arises when popularity is so important that the social multiplier exceeds unity in some intervals of price and other variables.

When $m > 1$, the sign of the relation in equation (9.2) between the aggregate demand for Q and a common variable appears to change from what the sign would be without such strong interactions. However, what really happens is that aggregate demand is unstable when $m > 1$. Every increase in aggregate demand raises everyone's demand by more than the initial increase, and so demand would increase in a continuing upward spiral.

Consider the diagram in Figure 9.1, which shows the aggregate demand for good Q as a function of its price. In the two intervals where the demand function is negatively sloped, the social multiplier m may be positive but must be less than unity. In the single interval where the function is positively sloped, $m > 1$, and $m = 1$ at the two turning points where the function is infinitely elastic.

Notice that a shift between the stable competitive equilibria at Q_l and Q_h involves an increase in both quantity and price, even though

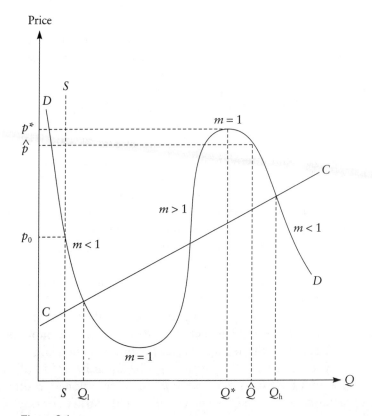

Figure 9.1

they are on the same demand function. Teenagers may commit a lot of crimes even though the rewards are low (the price of crime is high) because their peers are committing many crimes, or they may commit few crimes even though the rewards are high because their peers are not committing many crimes. The Japanese may smoke more cigarettes per capita than Americans, even though cigarettes are much more expensive in Japan, because social pressures to smoke are still strong there, whereas social pressures in the United States are now strongly opposed to smoking.

The positive slope in Figure 9.1, where $m > 1$, does not mean that demand in that interval rises as the price of this good increases, but rather that each household's willingness to pay for this good increases greatly as other households are consuming more of the good. When the social multiplier exceeds unity, an increase in aggregate quantity demanded by, say, 10 percent, perhaps due to a fall in price, induces through social interactions a further increase in aggregate quantity demanded by more than 10 percent, which induces a still larger increase in demand, and so forth. In other words, demand is unstable in this interval, and explodes up or down in response even to small shocks.

Therefore, an equilibrium in or near such an unstable region is vulnerable to small shocks that cause large changes in the popularity of the good. We believe this explains why popularity is so important to fads, and why fads involve unstable equilibria.

Previous chapters demonstrate that the effects of popularity and other forms of social interactions on prices and quantities depend on supply as well as demand conditions. We now show that monopolists have a profit incentive to move toward regions of unstable demand.

Assume first that a monopolist has a fixed number of units to sell in each period. This supply curve is given by SS in Figure 9.1, which intersects the demand function on its first negatively sloped section. With a conventional demand function that is everywhere negatively sloped, and with positive marginal revenue at S, the monopolist would sell S units at the price p_0 on the demand function.

However, that is not the profit-maximizing equilibrium with highly popular goods of the type depicted in this figure. The monopolist would be better off with the higher price p^* and the much larger quantity demanded, given by Q^*. Although the quantity sold still only equals S, so that the excess demand at p^* must be rationed, profits are much greater at (p^*, S) than at the conventional market clearing price (p_0, S) since p^* is much above p_0.

The equilibrium at (p^*, Q^*) has the right properties for a faddish good since it is *completely* unstable for *all* negative shocks to demand, no matter how small. A small decline in quantity demanded at that point encourages still further declines in demand through a social multiplier that exceeds one. This encourages additional declines until demand for this good eventually becomes almost extinct.

Of course, if demand falls almost to 0 from Q^*, the monopolist may have to settle for the more conventional equilibrium at (p_0, S). Moreover, a monopolist would anticipate the vulnerability to small shocks at (p^*, Q^*), and might set a somewhat lower price of $\hat{p}$ with the larger demand of $\hat{Q}$. Profits are smaller with $\hat{p}$ and the equilibrium $(\hat{p}, \hat{Q})$ is still vulnerable to negative shocks, but the shocks must be large enough to push demand below Q^*.

Monopolists trade off the advantages of higher prices with very unstable demand, and lower prices with locally stable demand. Still, in this case, monopolists would tend to locate in demand regions that are vulnerable to negative shocks to quantity because they want to take advantage of the rising willingness to pay of consumers in regions of rising demand curves.

This analysis can be generalized to include production and variable supply. A monopolist with constant costs of producing additional output, given by CC in Figure 9.2, has a local profit-maximizing position at (p_0, Q_0). However, this is not a global maximum because the section of rising willingness to pay has rising marginal revenue from larger output. The global profit-maximizing position has price equal to p^* and quantity equal to Q^*. There is no rationing of output with variable supply, but demand is still leftward unstable for sufficiently large negative shocks.

At any moment, particular restaurants, rock stars, sports, clothing styles, books, and other activities are popular and considered "in" or "cool," even when they are expensive. Some luck is necessary to become "in" and popular since demand may be vigorous only because each consumer expects other consumers to want the product. A good explanation of this analysis is in the *Economist* (1992a, p. 67).

But luck can also turn against an "in" restaurant, star, and so on, because such socially generated success is fickle and can readily produce failure. We have seen that any negative shock to demand at the equilibrium (p^*, Q^*) in Figure 9.1 sets in motion cumulative responses that kick demand at p^* in Figure 9.1 all the way down to zero. Perhaps a rumor spreads that a popular drug may be lethal, famous people stop go-

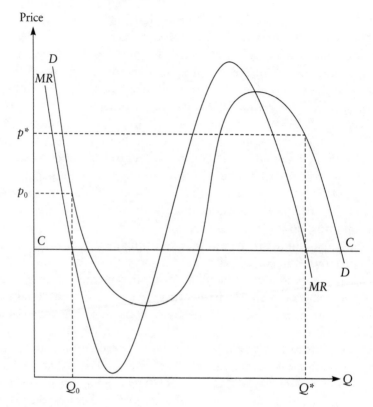

Figure 9.2

ing to a particular restaurant, or an athlete endorsing a product is arrested for battering his wife. At this point, there is a large excess supply rather than excess demand, so that the profit-maximizing price would then be much lower than p^*.

Unlike the "in" equilibrium, being "out" is stable, at least locally, so that small positive or negative shocks to demand in the interval where demand is negatively sloped do not cause cumulative increases in demand. In this way, social reinforcement and the social multiplier explains not only why fads seldom remain "in" and "cool" but also why it is so much harder to go from being "out" to being "in" than visa versa.

An excellent example of the importance of social reinforcement to success is the book on the universe *A Brief History of Time,* by the well-known, physically handicapped astrophysicist Stephen Hawking

(1988). This book sold over one million copies, although it is very hard going even for physicists, and only a tiny fraction of persons who own it can understand the discussion. Why did such a difficult book become so popular? Presumably, it became prestigious not to read it, but to display a copy on one's coffee table!

The experience with misprinted copies documents our assertion that few people read the book. Not long after publication it was discovered that the first 35,000 copies had serious misprints. Yet although the publisher offered to replace misprinted versions with corrected ones, no bookstore or individual bothered to accept this offer; apparently, bookstores went on selling misprinted copies along with corrected ones (this episode is discussed in *Lingua Franca*, 1992).

For every blockbuster success like *A Brief History of Time*, hundreds of books do much worse than expected since book sales are difficult to forecast: a few become big hits, while most fail to cover costs. Often, the success or failure of a book is due to the spread of favorable or unfavorable opinions from reviewers and other prominent readers. Sometimes, the main information that drives sales is simply that a book is popular, which is why being number one on a major bestseller list is so important (*Wall Street Journal*, 1995, p. B1). Indeed, some publishers have found ways to boost artificially the sales ranking of their books to achieve a high position on such lists.

Expensive sneakers and gold chains appeal to very different education and social groups than Hawking's book does, yet they too are popular and "in." The most prestigious sneaker line, the Nike Air Jordans, sells for over $100; some patent leather models cost almost $200 (see *New York Times*, 1996, p. B1). These expensive sneakers mainly attract poor ghetto teenagers who obviously are strapped to find the resources to pay for them. The musical "Bobos" treats a ghetto youth who sells drugs to get money to buy prestigious sneakers (*New York Times*, 1993a, p. 12).

Our analysis of fads assumes that social demand depends not on actual consumption but on *desired* consumption, even though demand may be rationed and some individuals may not be able to fully satisfy their desires. This is often a reasonable assumption, since demand for certain goods depends more on their *popularity* than on actual consumption. Indeed, as Groucho Marx recognized years ago in his quip that he would not join any club that would accept him as a member, a good may become more popular precisely because it is hard to get.

Indeed, for producers, the publicity given to efforts to buy their goods can be excellent and profitable advertising. They might even intentionally ration sales of some of their goods if the publicity this generates raises future demand for these goods, or raises demand for other goods that they sell. In this case, rationing is a form of advertising that makes some goods more popular. For example, although Air Jordan sneakers are quite expensive, they have been in short supply, apparently intentionally kept that way by Nike (*New York Times*, 1996, p. B1). The pricing by Nike of Air Jordans to maintain persistent excess demand suggests that the favorable publicity from rationing a prestige line raises demand for other Nike products.

3. Fashions

Part II has shown that elites and other leaders use various barriers to separate their behavior from others', including limits on the number of houses in neighborhoods where they live, the high cost of the top-quality goods they buy, and the limited markets for expensive trademarked products and collectibles. Followers may try to overcome these barriers by buying cheaper copies of originals and trademarked goods, and even by buying counterfeit merchandise.

The creation and destruction of these barriers explain why what is "fashionable" does not last and often has a short life span. After a while, cheaper versions of fashionable objects and activities become available to followers. Once this happens, entrepreneurs then try to find new objects, goods, and activities that can attract leaders but not followers. Leaders then shift from what was formerly fashionable to newer fashions.

In other words, leaders usually only have *temporarily* protected markets because followers eventually begin to catch up to the leaders. Alert leaders recognize that their distinctive behavior is only temporary, and are on the lookout for new ways to be distinguished from the followers who are closing the gap in behavior. Such leaders are rewarded for finding these opportunities by gaining further distinction as fashion-setters who discover objects and behavior that appeal mainly to their peers.

Chapters 6 and 7 have shown how copies and counterfeits can break down barriers between leaders and followers. We now consider the dynamics related to the decline in pricing over time of new goods. Assume a high initial cost per unit of a new good, given by c_n in Figure 9.3, and that the industry is competitive, so that market price $p_n = c_n$. At that

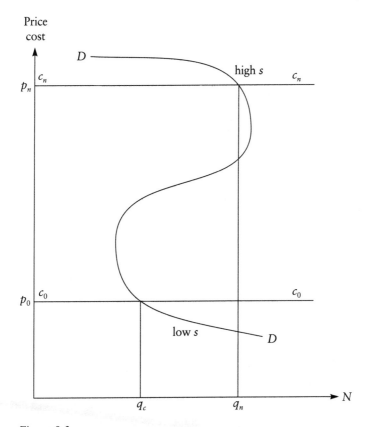

Figure 9.3

high price, we assume that most consumers are leaders; which means that s, the share of leaders in total consumption, is close to one.

Followers enter at lower prices, so that s will fall as price falls. As more followers consume the product at lower prices, this reduces the demand of *both* leaders and followers. The result could be a positively sloped section of the aggregate demand curve, DD in Figure 9.3, in an interval where s falls sharply at lower prices. When price is sufficiently low, most leaders have left the market, s is low, and the demand curve is again negatively sloped.

Over time, the cost of producing this good falls because of learning by doing and other technological improvements in its production. In Figure 9.3, costs eventually fall from c_n to c_0, where they remain stationary relative to average production costs in the economy. Initially the fall in costs and prices expands consumption, since DD is negatively sloped in the region near c_n. Leaders would expand their consumption and some followers are induced by lower prices to consume this good. Eventually, however, as prices continue to fall over time, consumption declines rather than increases because leaders and some followers leave the market as followers become increasingly dominant.

Indeed, demand might suddenly collapse when prices enter the backward-bending section of DD, because equilibria along that section are not stable. In Figure 9.3, consumption at the long-run equilibrium with $p = c_0$ is less than at the equilibrium when the good is new (p_n, q_n).

In this example, consumption shifts from leaders to followers as new goods age. At the long-run equilibrium in Figure 9.3, few leaders remain because most of them bailed out of this market after many followers entered. Leaders shift to newly discovered goods, and to other fashionable activities with high enough prices or other barriers to keep out most followers, at least for a while. The maturation process eventually also begins for these newer goods and activities; prices fall as technology improves, and followers enter the market.

This maturation process can be delayed by patents, trademarks, and other factors that give producers monopoly positions. Even when costs fall, a monopolist may maintain high prices because demand is inelastic in regions where leaders and some followers exit as followers enter. In Figure 9.3, a monopolist would charge a price near p_n even though costs are much lower, at c_0.

But even this monopoly power gets eroded over time as profits encourage copies and other substitutes that appeal to followers. Such increasing competition discourages consumption by leaders as these goods get "polluted" with substitutes. Eventually, leaders switch to products with better-"protected" markets.

Fashions change in this analysis not because leaders have a desire for change built into their preferences, although that sometimes is important. Rather, their interest in new fashions comes from an unchanging desire for distinction—a desire to behave differently from the masses. It is the erosion over time of high prices and other barriers to mass consumption that forces leaders to search for new ways to distinguish themselves.

Particular behavior is "fashionable" if it distinguishes leaders from followers only temporarily. In our analysis, fashionable behavior is initially too expensive for followers, but sometimes followers are not aware of what leaders are doing, or they are unable to adjust their behavior quickly to imitate that of leaders. Such lags in behavior are essential to the early model of fashion cycles by Karni and Schmeidler (1990); but these lags are superimposed on behavior rather than being an internal part of their modeling.

Price declines over time are part of our modeling of the supply of new goods, designs, and processes because these generate rapid technological improvements and competition from cheaper copies. Many commentators on fashion have recognized that newness plays an important role in fashion "cycles." They have stressed the attractions of novelty to elites, but they have ignored the high prices of new products which temporarily erect barriers between leaders and followers. However, these barriers fall over time as technological improvements and increased competition lower prices and attract followers.

The Formation of Norms and Values

1. Introduction

Previous chapters have shown how an individual's preferences and other determinants of behavior are affected by the behavior of others, sometimes especially that by elites and other leaders. Some forms of common behavior are extremely valuable to a group, but they are not always valuable to individual members. For example, people who interact with a person known to be honest can rely on her behavior without having to closely supervise her.

But while they benefit, she may be hurt at times by her honesty if it prevents her from taking advantage of opportunities that require dishonest behavior. The privately optimal behavior may be honesty when that pays and dishonesty when that pays, but this flexibility may also hurt her if others will not deal with her because she is not trustworthy.

If flexibility with regard to, say, honest behavior is harmful on balance because the disadvantages from being distrusted outweigh the opportunities to benefit from dishonesty, a person would prefer to be committed to honesty by "hardwiring." One way to accomplish this is to have the "taste" for honesty built into preferences. Then preferences would commit a person to act honestly even when honesty does not "pay," so that other persons would be willing to trust people with these hardwired preferences.

Since people cannot simply "choose" the values they want, they must get values hardwired into preferences for them to be effective. This chapter gives several examples of ways that norms and values get built into preferences: by teaching and preaching in schools, churches, and at home, and by reinforcement of past behavior through habits and other recursive influences. Section 2 shows how the family and "interest" groups use their influence over the formation of preferences, especially among children, to instill various ethical and other norms and values, such as support of elderly parents in need, or respect for private property.

Even for adults, the force of habit and repetition means that people can in essence "choose" their preferences by making choices now with an eye toward the effect on their values and other preferences in the future. In particular, if habit reinforces present behavior, they may become more committed to honest behavior by acting honestly now.

Section 3 analyzes how habits and other influences of past experiences on behavior make it easier to hardwire into preferences a willingness to cooperate, respect for a government constitution, and other values and norms. For example, if several persons are interacting over time, they might all benefit if they act cooperatively for a while, and only "defect" from cooperation later on. But if behavior is strongly habitual, cooperative actions, even if only for a little while, would build in a taste for further cooperation that could be maintained even when defection looks profitable. Section 3 sketches out a rigorous model of such a process.

2. Influences over the Formation of Norms

Interest Group Creation of Norms

To show how some groups may influence the norms of others, even when all behavior is voluntary, assume that the population is divided into two groups, R and M. We further assume (this analysis follows that in Becker, 1996) that only the group R—possibly standing for "rich"—can spend resources collectively to promote the interests of its members. Perhaps R is relatively small, which enables R to overcome the tendency of its members to free ride on the efforts of other members, or members of R are related through intermarriage. Assume too that the interests of R and M conflict, so that a promotion of R's interests generally harms M's.

Norms and values about the sanctity of life, respect for private property, and so on are promoted by R through influencing what is taught in institutions like churches or schools—we call all of them "churches."

We assume that no one is required to attend these institutions, so those who do must believe they gain from doing so. In particular, M would not attend churches where they acquire norms promoted by R that lower M's utility unless they are sufficiently compensated in other ways. Otherwise, M would not go to church, or would find churches that promote more congenial values.

R subsidizes clergy, buildings, and other church expenses if they promote norms that are favorable to R, such as the interest of rich families in fostering respect for private property. These subsidies can make churches that promote norms favorable to R also attractive to M, even when M is harmed by these norms. To formalize this, write the utility function of members of M as

$$(10.1) \qquad\qquad U = U(X, N, Y),$$

where X are the private goods obtained by "church" attendance—such as faith and support during crises, or learning how to read and write—N are the norms promoted by these churches, and Y are other goods.

We assume $\partial U/\partial N < 0$ to indicate that churches promote norms which harm M. But M must absorb N to get the X's produced by churches, the same way that consumers often must absorb advertising to get the television programming supported by advertisers. If R subsidizes the production of X that lowers its cost to M by $S(N)$, and if the monetary equivalent of the loss to M from absorbing N norms equals $L(N)$, M would not be made worse off by attending churches that produce N norms if

$$(10.2) \qquad\qquad S(N) - L(N) \geq 0.$$

Given N, R would reduce S to the minimum level necessary to attract M, which is the loss to M from these norms. Hence one equilibrium condition is

$$(10.3) \qquad\qquad S(N) = L(N).$$

If $C(N)$ is the cost to R of producing N, then R would have to spend $S(N) + C(N)$ to get M to accept N. R would be willing to spend this much on N if R gains at least as much. Therefore, an equilibrium condition for R is:

(10.4) $$G(N) \geq S(N) + C(N),$$

where $G(N)$ is the gain to R from N.

By equation (10.3), this equation can be written as

(10.5) $$G(N) \geq L(N) + C(N).$$

This last equation shows that the gain to R must exceed the loss to M by enough to cover the cost, C, of producing norms favorable to R. *No one* is harmed when these norms become part of M's (and perhaps R's) preferences, because M voluntarily accept R as part of their preferences. M receive enough compensation for absorbing N to make the absorption worthwhile, and R would not promote N unless they too were made better off, or at least no worse off.

Our analysis has a "functionalist" flavor because these norms help the group R without hurting other groups. Of course, this result is not surprising since mutual benefit is the property of any voluntary "trade," and M voluntarily accepts these norms. However, the norms produced in our analysis are *biased* in favor of R since they are the only group that is assumed to be able to act collectively. Not *all* "functional" norms are produced, since norms that hurt R and benefit M may not evolve as long as M cannot act effectively as a group.

Children's Support of Elderly Parents

The benefit-cost calculation is looser when exchange is not voluntary, and some persons *must* be exposed to the influence of others. This is the situation when schooling is compulsory, and schools teach values that may promote the interests of particular groups—such as the rich, trade unions, business, gays, or others (see Bowles and Gintis, 1976; Lott, 1990) at possibly great cost to other groups. But families hurt by these teachings can choose not to send their children to school, even if it is compulsory and they face a threat of punishment.

A more extreme example of involuntary association is the rearing of children by their parents. Young children have little choice but to be exposed to the norms and values promoted by their parents, although evolution has also provided children with various defenses against their parents' influence. Altruistic as well as selfish parents may use their control over the rearing of children to hardwire a desire to help parents into their children's preferences, even when that hurts children. We illustrate this process with the formation of the "norm" for children to help elderly parents.

To develop this analysis, assume the life cycle is divided into three periods: childhood, middle age, and old age. Individuals work only during middle age, so that they must accumulate various "assets" to support them in their old age. Either they can accumulate land and other tangible assets, or they can expect to rely on support from their children (this model is taken from Becker, 1993).

Parents have a given number of children at the beginning of middle age, and they spend the resources X and Y in rearing their children during this period of their life. They also spend Z_{mp} and Z_{op} on their own consumption during middle and old age, respectively, while k_c are bequests to children, R_k is the return on savings, and A_p the value of all resources, including discounted earnings, at the beginning of middle age.

Y is devoted to raising children's consumption and utility, and possibly also their human capital. In contrast, the purpose of X is to create a "norm" or "value" among the children when they become adults that induces them to help their elderly parents if they need help. Parents might make children feel guilt or gratitude toward them, which could lower the utility of children when they become adults at the same time that it makes them more willing to help their parents.

Combining these various ways for parents to spend, and assuming a perfect market in assets and no uncertainty, the budget constraint of parents at the beginning of their middle age is

$$(10.6) \qquad Z_{mp} + X + Y + \frac{Z_{op}}{R_k} + \frac{k_c}{R_k} = A_p + G/R_k,$$

where G is the old-age support from children. We assume that future income is discounted at the rate R_k because some capital is accumulated for old age, but this assumption is not necessary. We assume, to simplify, that investment in children starts with this generation.

The discounted utility function of parents at the beginning of their middle age is assumed to be

$$(10.7) \qquad V_p = u_{mp} + \beta u_{op} + \beta a V_c,$$

where u_m and u_o are the utility functions at middle and old age, β is the discount rate, and a is the degree of altruism toward children. Parents are selfish if $a = 0$, and their degree of altruism rises as a increases. To simplify the presentation, we assume that the process begins with these parents, so they do not feel any guilt and do not support their parents.

The utility function of middle-aged children equals

$$(10.8) \qquad V_c = u_{mc} + h(Y) - g(X, G) + \beta u_{oc} + \beta a V_{gc},$$

where V_{gc} is the utility of the grandchildren of the parents, and $h(Y)$ and $g(X, G)$ are different effects of early childhood experiences on adult utilities. The function g measures the degree of guilt or gratitude of children due to parental spending of X on them when they were children.

This utility function assumes that greater guilt lowers adult utility. We also assume that an increase in X raises guilt, so that $g_x > 0$. Why would altruistic parents ($a > 0$) intentionally use scarce resources ($X > 0$) to lower the utility of their children? The answer must be that guilty children provide offsetting advantages to parents. These advantages are found in the effect of guilt on willingness to support elderly parents. Since G is the amount of support, we assume that $\partial g/\partial G = g_G < 0$, and that $g_{Gx} < 0$. Greater support from children reduces their guilt, and greater spending by parents on making children guilty, X, raises the marginal reduction in the guilt of children from spending more on their elderly parents.

Parents choose the optimal spending on their own consumption and their children. The FOC for Y is straightforward:

$$(10.9) \qquad \beta a h_y \le v_p,$$

where v_p is the marginal utility of wealth to parents, and we ignore any utility during childhood. If parents are sufficiently altruistic, equation (10.9) is a strict equality.

The FOC for X is more interesting, for as we have suggested, even very altruistic parents may want to lower the utility of their children if that induces enough old-age support. The total effect of a change in X on parental utility is given by the middle terms in the following FOC:

$$(10.10) \qquad \frac{dV_p}{dX} = \beta(u'_{op} - au'_{mc}) \frac{dG}{dX} - \frac{\beta a dg}{dX} \le v_p,$$

with equality if $X > 0$.

The term dG/dX gives the induced change in old-age support from an increase in guilt-creating spending, and dg/dX gives the total change in guilt of children, including any induced change in G.

The term in parentheses is zero if parents are sufficiently altruistic to give bequests to children, for then the marginal utility to parents from old-age consumption must equal the marginal utility to parents from increased consumption by their children. Clearly, parents giving bequests would not want old-age support from children, for the middle term of equation (10.10) would then be negative. These parents have no incentive to make their children feel guilty, for parents who do not want old-age support from their children, and who also care about the well-being of their children, have no incentive to create utility-lowering guilt among their children.

If parents do not give bequests and want old-age support, the term in parentheses must be positive. These parents get more marginal utility from old-age consumption than they get from the consumption of their children. They would be willing to lower their children's utility by making them more guilty if the value to parents of the additional old-age support exceeds the loss to parents from guiltier children. In particular, selfish parents ($a = 0$) might be very willing to spend a lot on making their children guiltier.

In this case, old-age support by children is a "norm" enforced entirely by each set of parents' actions that generate preferences of their own children to help out their elderly parents. Before we bring into the analysis the influences of one family on another, consider a few interesting implications of the simpler analysis.

As countries have developed and become wealthier, the trend has been away from children's support of parents toward parental support of children through investments in human capital and bequests. This development has been associated with a trend away from "closely knit" families. According to our analysis, children and other relatives are no longer as close to one another as in the past because parents have less to gain from promoting gratitude, guilt, and other characteristics of children that encourage them to provide generous old-age support.

These considerations imply that poorer and middle-class families may be closer and feel greater obligations to one another than richer families do. For families that are more likely to want support from their children in old age invest more in maintaining a close relation with their children.

Pay as you go (PAYG) government social security programs, which began at the end of the nineteenth century in Germany, have an independent effect on parental investments in children's guilt and related attitudes. Since PAYG pensions raise the consumption of retired persons, these pensions reduce the marginal utility to the elderly from support by their children. As a result, PAYG social security also weakens parents' incentives to invest in encouraging children to help them out when they become old.

Children may help support their elderly parents not only because they feel gratitude or guilt but also because of the influence on their preferences of peers who are helping their parents. If children deviated from what the others do, they would be considered "uncaring," and would tend to lose status and acceptance.

Therefore, spending on parents depends not only on guilt and gratitude, as in equation (10.8), but also on peer pressure. In turn, pressure on children in the ith family depends on the support provided by peers, G^*, and the difference between G^* and the support provided by these children, G^i. Marginal peer pressure on children to support their parents weakens with increases in the gap between what they are doing and what their peers are doing.

The result of parental actions and peer pressure is a parental support function that is increasing in parental actions and also in these two dimensions of peer pressure. For simplicity, we assume that peer effects are separable from parent-created effects:

(10.11) $$G^i = F^i(X^i) + H^i(G^* - G^i, G^*), \quad \text{with } F^{i\prime} > 0,$$

and both partial derivatives of H are positive. If all families in the same peer group are identical, in equilibrium, $G^i = G^*$ for all i.

If $H(0, 0) = 0$, then $H(0, G^*) > 0$ when $G^* > 0$ since $H_2 > 0$. Therefore, in equilibrium, social pressure must increase the support by children to their elderly parents, *given* the spending by parents on guilt creation, since

(10.12) $$G^i = F^i(X^i) + H^i(0, G^*) > F^i(X^i).$$

However, spending by parents is not independent of the effects of peer pressure; indeed, such pressure reduces parental spending on generating support from children. The explanation is that peer pressure reduces the effect of parental spending on children's giving, which induces parents to partially free ride on the spending of other parents. To see this, totally differentiating equation (10.11) with respect to X^i—holding G^* fixed—and collecting terms:

$$(10.13) \qquad \frac{dG^i}{dX^i} = \frac{F^{i\prime}}{1 + H_1^i} < F^{i\prime}.$$

Peer pressure reduces the gain from inducing support by one's children because this pressure is weakened when support in the family rises relative to that in peer families. The stronger is H_1—the effect on giving by children in the ith family of increases in the gap between giving by other children and their own giving—the weaker the incentive for the ith parents to devote much resources to inducing support from their children. Indeed, the induced decline in spending by each family from peer pressure could be so strong that *total* giving by children is reduced, despite equation (10.12).

A potential conflict between family actions and peer pressure is found in all norms that result from both peer pressure and actions that families take on their own. This conflict materializes if the peer pressure on a particular family is weaker when that family is doing relatively more compared with its peers. This conflict lowers the effect of the family's actions on the strength of these norms. In fact, as we have seen with old-age support, such "free riding" induced by peer pressure could be so powerful that peer pressure could actually *weaken* the very norms it appears to be strengthening.

3. Habits and the Formation of Norms

Veneration of Constitutions

Chapter 2 shows that habits and other recursive behavior can anchor a particular market equilibrium in social markets with multiplicity of equilibria. In essence, habits provide an anchor by strengthening the forces making for persistence in behavior. That chapter models the effects of preferences that depend not only on what others are doing but also on a person's own past activities and experiences.

By strengthening persistence, habits increase the durability and range of norms and other values. This role of habits was indirectly quite prominent in the famous dispute between James Madison and Thomas Jefferson over the properties of the U.S. Constitution. Jefferson argued during the debates over its ratification that constitutions should have only *temporary* authority, so that future generations could rewrite them to take account of important changes in circumstances.

On the surface, Jefferson's argument is attractive since enormous changes in technology, economic conditions, and social pressures are difficult to fit into constitutions written decades and centuries ago. And yet the founding fathers were wise not to heed Jefferson's advice. Constitutions need to be obeyed and respected—the world is filled with wonderful constitutions that are ignored or evaded. Indeed, Argentina, Brazil, and Peru altered their constitutions only a few years after they were drafted to allow second and third terms for popular presidents.

James Madison (1961) bluntly replied to Jefferson in the Federalist Papers that a temporary constitution for the new United States would be a major disaster. He argued that constitutions command great allegiance only after they have survived for a long time. The rewriting of constitutions by each new generation advocated by Jefferson would deprive a constitution of "that veneration, which time bestows on everything, and without which perhaps the wisest and freest governments would not posses the requisite stability" (Madison, 1961, p. 340).

Two centuries later, Madison's claims about the importance of time and habit in gaining support for a constitution receives confirmation from the idolatry that most Americans give to the Constitution. Madison was right and Jefferson was wrong; attitudes and behavior become much firmer after they have continued for decades and centuries since habit capital takes time to build up. Once attitudes have acquired strong allegiance, they can be replaced only with great difficulty.

A Propensity to Cooperate: A Formal Model

An example can show more systematically how the interaction of habits and the behavior of others creates "norms" that could not be created without habitual behavior. The example analyzes the propensity to cooperate even when cooperation does not appear to promote narrow self-interest, although the principles illustrated apply to many other norms as well (this discussion is based on the formal analysis in Becker and Madrigal, 1998).

We consider repeated prisoners' dilemma games because they illustrate cleanly the difficulty of getting cooperation without habits. In particular, we assume that two persons engage in repeated one-period games where they can choose one of only two strategies, C and D. If they both choose C—the "cooperative" strategy—the payoff to each is much higher than if they both choose D—the selfish "defection" strategy. However, if one of them chooses C, the other receives a higher pay-off by choosing D rather than C.

If they repeat this game only a finite number of times, the usual back-ward induction argument appears to prove that they would defect at the last play—each would play D then—since cooperation there cannot induce future cooperation. But defection then induces defection at the next-to-last play, and eventually at all earlier plays, so that the only per-fect equilibrium is defection at all plays by both players. Both would appear to choose D at all stages despite the gains to both from coopera-tion.

However, this well-known and apparently conclusive argument de-pends not only on the finiteness of plays but also on strong assumptions about preferences. Even if everyone is selfish, a crucial assumption is also that utilities from any play depend *only* on the payoffs from that play, so that preferences are separable over time. But the backward in-duction argument collapses if behavior is strongly habitual, so that a person's utility depends also on his previous behavior.

To see this, consider incentives on the last play to cooperate if a per-son's utility will be greater if he continues with the choices—either D or C—that he made more frequently in the past. For example, if he tended to cooperate (choose C) in the past, other things the same, he will would get more utility if he continues to cooperate because of the force of habits. Of course, his payoff on the last play would be less from co-operation than from defection, but the utility advantage of continuing to cooperate may be worth more to him than the reduction in the last period's payoff. If so, he continues to cooperate on the last play, even if his opponent does not, and even though he receives a smaller payoff.

This implies that if habitual behavior provides enough utility, coop-eration on all plays may be a subgame perfect equilibrium, despite the finite number of repeated plays. In this case, habits would support the "norm" of cooperation, even when cooperation does not "pay," and even when this norm could not be supported without a powerful hold of habit on behavior. This example illustrates that habits not only help choose the equilibrium when there are many potential equilibria, but may also add to the number of equilibria.

The analysis becomes more interesting when a group of individuals interact through a set of two-person repeated plays of such games. Sup-pose that each member of a sizable "peer" group plays a finite number of identical games against an opponent chosen at random from this group. At the end of their series of plays, they get new opponents again chosen at random from this set.

Becker and Madrigal (1998) assume that the utility of each player is greater when his play conforms with his previous choices, including those with prior opponents. In order not to bias the process toward cooperation by assumptions about preferences, Becker and Madrigal assume that the habitual utility from conforming to past defection play (choosing D's) is just as strong as the utility from conforming to past cooperative play (choosing C's). Everyone starts out at the beginning of the games with utility that depends only on current payoffs, but each is forward looking and knows his preferences are habitual.

Players are assumed not to know anything about the prior plays of new opponents, but they do know the distribution of prior plays in the set of all potential opponents. Becker and Madrigal show why there may be an evolution toward the "norm" to cooperate in a group of players with these habitual preferences. Although they assume fully symmetrical habitual gains from either cooperation or defection, the nature of the payoffs from prisoners' dilemma games still imparts a "bias" in play toward cooperation. For since players know that everyone's preferences have a habitual component, they know that cooperation can be supported, even in a finite number of games. Consequently, players have an incentive to start out in a new series of games by cooperating, especially when most players have cooperated in the past, since their opponents may continue to cooperate if they cooperate.

By a "bias" toward cooperation, we mean that with reasonable values for the strength of habitual behavior, time preference, payoffs from cooperation and defection, and other parameters, there can be an evolution over time toward the "norm" of cooperation by a large majority of the players. Some players would continue to defect from the norm to take advantage of the gain from defection when most opponents cooperate. Still, most may cooperate since they recognize that most of their opponents are also likely to cooperate, especially if they do.

Although defection on all plays continues to be a subgame perfect equilibrium, there are also equilibria with many parameter values that have overwhelming allegiance to the cooperative norm. This norm evolves not from social pressure by peers and others—as in the discussion of the norm to help elderly parents—but from habitual behavior and the selfish advantages of cooperating with opponents.

Although we have taken the importance of habitual behavior as given, this analysis may even help explain the evolution of human preferences toward heavy reliance on habit. Habit raises efficiency if past behavior restrains participants' choices toward contributing to overall efficiency. However, this argument implies that only *moderately* strong habitual behavior has an evolutionary advantage. If the power of habit is too strong, opponents can take advantage of an excessively strong commitment to continue with the choices made in the past, such as a tendency to cooperate simply because of past cooperation. There must still be some threat to punish most opponents if they behave too opportunistically.

References / Index

References

Altonji, Joseph G., Fumio Hayashi, and Laurence J. Kotlikoff. 1997. Parental altruism and inter vivos transfers: Theory and evidence. *Journal of Political Economy* 105, no. 6 (December): 1121–66.

Arrow, Kenneth J., and Robert C. Lind. 1970. Uncertainty and the evaluation of public investment decisions. *American Economic Review* 60, no. 3 (June): 364–378.

Bagwell, Laurie Simon, and Douglas B. Bernheim. 1996. Veblen effects in a theory of conspicuous consumption. *American Economic Review* 86, no. 3 (June): 349–373.

Balakrishnan, T. R., Evelyne Lapierre-Adamczyk, and Karol K. Krotki. 1993. *Family and childbearing in Canada: A demographic analysis*. Toronto: University of Toronto Press.

Becker, Gary S. 1957 (1971). *The economics of discrimination*. Chicago: University of Chicago Press.

——— 1968. Crime and punishment: An economic approach. *Journal of Political Economy* 76, no. 2 (March–April): 169–217.

——— 1981. Altruism in the family and selfishness in the marketplace. *Economica* 48, no. 189 (February): 1–15.

——— 1991. *A treatise on the family*. Cambridge, Mass.: Harvard University Press.

——— 1993. Nobel lecture: The economic way of looking at behavior. *Journal of Political Economy* 101, no. 3 (June): 385–409.

——— 1996. *Accounting for tastes*. Cambridge, Mass.: Harvard University Press.

Becker, Gary S., Elisabeth M. Landes, and Robert T. Michael. 1977. An economic analysis of marital instability. *Journal of Political Economy* 85, no. 6 (December): 1141–87.

Becker, Gary S., and Vicente Madrigal. 1998. The formation of values with habitual behavior. Manuscript. University of Chicago.

Becker, Gary S., and Kevin M. Murphy. 1988. A theory of rational addiction. *Journal of Political Economy* 96, no. 4 (August): 675–700.

——— 1994. The sorting of individuals into categories when tastes and productivity depend on the composition of members. Manuscript. University of Chicago.

Becker, Gary S., Kevin M. Murphy, and Iván Werning. 2000. Status, lotteries, and inequality. Manuscript. University of Chicago.

Benabou, Roland. 1993. Workings of a city: Location, education, and production. *Quarterly Journal of Economics* 108, no. 3 (August): 619–652.

——— 1996a. Equity and efficiency in human capital investment: The local connection. *Review of Economic Studies* 63, no. 2: 237–264.

——— 1996b. Heterogeneity, stratification, and growth: Macroeconomic implications of community structure and school finance. *American Economic Review* 86, no. 3 (June): 584–609.

Bikhchandani, Sushil, David Hirshleifer, and Ivo Welch. 1992. A theory of fads, fashion, custom, and cultural change in informational cascades. *Journal of Political Economy* 100, no. 5 (October): 992–1026.

Bongarts, John, and Susan C. Watkins. 1996. Social interactions and contemporary fertility transitions. *Population and Development Review* 22, no. 4 (December): 639–682.

Bowles, Samuel, and Herbert Gintis. 1976. *Schooling in capitalist America: Educational reform and the contradictions of economic life.* New York: Basic Books.

Brenner, Reuven. 1983. *History: The human gamble.* Chicago: University of Chicago Press.

Brock, William A., and Steven N. Durlauf. 1995. *Discrete choice with social interactions,* I: *Theory.* National Bureau of Economic Research Working Paper 5921. October.

Brown v. Board of Education. 1954. 47 U.S. 294.

Browning, Martin, and Pierre A. Chiappori. 1998. Efficient intra-household allocations: A general characterization and empirical tests. *Econometrica* 66, no. 6 (November): 1241–78.

Carrington, William J., and Kenneth R. Troske. 1998a. Sex segregation in U.S. manufacturing. *Industrial and Labor Relations Review* 51, no. 3 (April): 445–464.

——— 1998b. Interfirm segregation and the black/white wage gap. *Journal of Labor Economics* 16, no. 2 (April 1998): 231–260.

Cho, In-Koo, and David M. Kreps. 1987. Signaling games and stable equilibria. *Quarterly Journal of Economics* 102, no. 2 (May): 179–221.

Cole, Harold L., George J. Mailath, and Andrew Postlewaite. 1992. Class system and the enforcement of social norms. *Journal of Public Economics* 70, no. 1 (October): 5–35.

Cole, Harold L., and Edward C. Prescott. 1997. Valuation equilibrium with clubs. *Journal of Economic Theory* 74, no. 1 (May): 19–39.

Coleman, James S. 1961. *The adolescent society: The social life of a teenager and its impact on education.* New York: Free Press of Glencoe.

——— 1990. *Foundations of social theory.* Cambridge: Belknap Press of Harvard University Press.

Cutler, David M., Edward L. Glaeser, and Jacob L. Vidgor. 1999. The rise and decline of the American ghetto. *Journal of Political Economy* 107, no. 3 (June): 455–506.

Darwin, Charles. 1859. *On the origin of the species by means of natural selection; or, The preservation of favored races in the struggle for life.* London: J. Murray.

Deaton, Angus, and John Muelbauer. 1980. *Economics and consumer behavior.* Cambridge: Cambridge University Press.

De Bartolome, Charles A. M. 1990. Equilibrium and inefficiency in a community model with peer group effects. *Journal of Political Economy* 98, no. 1 (February): 110–133.

Douglas, Mary. 1983. Identity: Personal and socio-cultural. *Uppsala Studies in Cultural Anthropology* 5: 35–46.

Drewianka, Scott. 1999. Social effects in marriage markets: Existence, magnitude, and nature. Ph.D. dissertation, Department of Economics, University of Chicago.

Duesenberry, James. 1960. Comment on "An economic analysis of fertility." In *Demographic and Economic Change in Developed Countries: A Conference of the Universities—National Bureau of Economic Research.* Princeton: Princeton University Press for the National Bureau of Economic Research.

Economist. 1992a. Why a queue? February 8, p. 67.

——— 1992b. The luxury-goods trade. December 26, 1992–January 8, 1993, pp. 95–98.

Fernandes, Ana Cristina de S. 1999. Familial preferences and economic choices: Does distribution matter? Ph.D. dissertation, Department of Economics, University of Chicago.

Fernández, Raquel, and Richard Rogerson. 1999. Sorting and long-run inequality. Manuscript. New York University.

Ferrari S.p.A. v. Roberts. 1991. 944 F.2d 1235 (6th Cir.).

Financial Times. 1998. Something new, something old—The show is the highlight of the year, and 100,000 visitors are expected. April 18, p. II.

Flanders, Stephanie, and Bruno Thiry. 1991. Who should get the champagne spoils? *Business Strategy Review* 2, no. 3 (Autumn): 91–111.

Frank, Robert H. 1985. *Choosing the right pond: Human behavior and the quest for status.* New York: Oxford University Press.

——— 1999. *Luxury fever: Why money fails to satisfy in an era of excess.* New York: Free Press.

Frey, Bruno S., and Werner W. Pommerehne. 1989. Art investment: An empirical inquiry. *Southern Economic Journal* 56, no. 2 (October): 396–409.

Friedman, Milton. 1953. Choice, chance, and the personal distribution of income. *Journal of Political Economy* 61, no. 4 (August): 277–290.

Gale, David, and Lloyd Shapley. 1962. College admissions and the stability of marriage. *American Mathematical Monthly* 69: 9–15.

Galenson, David W., and Bruce Weinberg. 2000. "Age and the quality of work: The case of modern American painters." *Journal of Political Economy* (August).

Gladwell, Malcolm. 2000. *The tipping point.* Boston: Little, Brown.

Glaeser, Edward L., Bruce Sacerdote, and José A. Scheinkman. 1996. Crime and social interactions. *Quarterly Journal of Economics* 111, no. 2 (May): 507–548.

Greeley, Andrew M. 1994. A religious revival in Russia? *Journal of the Scientific Study of Religion* 33, no. 3 (September): 253–272.

Grossbard-Shechtman, Shoshana. 1993. *On the economics of marriage: A theory of marriage, labor, and divorce.* Boulder: Westview Press.

Hawking, Stephen W. 1988. *A brief history of time: From the big bang to black holes.* London: Bantam.

Higgins, Richard S., and Paul H. Rubin. 1986. Counterfeit goods. *Journal of Law and Economics* 29, no. 2 (October): 211–230.

Hirsch, Fred. 1976. *Social limits to growth.* Cambridge, Mass.: Harvard University Press.

Iannaccone, Laurence R. 1998. Introduction to the Economics of Religion. *Journal of Economic Literature* 36, no. 3 (September): 1465–95.

Ichimura, Hideiko, and Jinyoung Kim. 1996. A model of fertility with selective and unselective abortions: A study of recent sex imbalance among newborn babies in Korea. Manuscript. State University of New York at Buffalo.

Karni, Edi, and David Schmeidler. 1990. Fixed preferences and changing tastes. *American Economic Review* 80, no. 2 (May): 262–267.

Kremer, Michael. 1997. How much does sorting increase inequality? *Quarterly Journal of Economics* 112, no. 1 (February): 115–139.

Landes, William M., and Richard A. Posner. 1987. Trademark law: An economic perspective. *Journal of Law and Economics* 30, no. 2 (October): 265–309.

—— 1996. The economics of legal disputes over the ownership of works of art and other collectibles. In Victor A. Ginsburgh and Pierre M. Menger, eds., *Economics of the arts: Selected essays,* pp. 177–219. Amsterdam: Elsevier Science B.V.

Lingua Franca. 1992. An extremely brief history of "A brief history of time." June/July, p. 23.

Lott, John R., Jr. 1990. An explanation for public provision of schooling: The importance of indoctrination. *Journal of Law and* Economics 33, no. 1 (April): 199–231.

Loury, Glenn. 1977. A dynamic theory of racial income differences. In Phyllis Wallace and Annette LaMond, eds., *Women, minorities, and employment discrimination,* pp. 153–188. Lexington, Mass.: Lexington Books.

Lundberg, Shelly, and Robert A. Pollak. 1996. Bargaining and distribution in marriage. *Journal of Economic Perspectives* 10, no. 4 (Fall): 139–158.

Madison, James. 1961. The Federalist No. 49. In Jacob E. Cook, ed., *The Federalist,* pp. 338–343. Middletown: Wesleyan University Press.

McElroy, Marjorie B., and Mary J. Horney. 1981. Nash-bargained household decisions: Toward a generalization of the theory of demand. *International Economic Review* 22, no. 2: 333–349.

Milgrom, Paul, and John Roberts. 1990. The economics of modern manufacturing: Technology, strategy, and organization. *American Economic Review* 80, no. 3 (June): 511–528.

Mulligan, Casey B. 1997. *Parental priorities and economic inequality.* Chicago: University of Chicago Press.

Mussa, Michael, and Sherwin Rosen. 1978. Monopoly and product quality. *Journal of Economic Theory* 18, no. 2 (August): 310–317.

New York Times. 1993a. A musical's question: What price sneakers? April 3, p. 12.

———— 1993b. Givenchy wins a major round in discount fight. September 4, p. 37.

———— 1996. A new Jordan sneaker inspires a frenetic run—A planned shoe shortage, at $115 a pair. July 4, p. B1.

Nussbaum, Bruce. 1998. The summer of wretched excess. *Business Week,* August 3, p. 35.

Plato. 1953. *The republic of Plato.* New York: Oxford University Press, 1953.

Posner, Richard A. 1992. *Sex and reason.* Cambridge, Mass.: Harvard University Press.

Robson, Arthur J. 1992. Status, the distribution of wealth, private and social attitudes to risk. *Econometrica* 60, no. 4 (July): 837–857.

Rosen, Sherwin. 1974. Hedonic prices and implicit market: Product differentiation in pure competition. *Journal of Political Economy* 82, no. 1 (January-February): 34–55.

———— 1981. The economics of superstars. *American Economic Review* 71, no. 5 (December): 845–858.

———— 1997. Manufactured inequality. *Journal of Labor Economics* 15, no. 2 (April): 186–196.

Roth, Alvin E., and Marilda A. O. Sotomayor. 1990. *Two-sided matching: A study in game-theoretic modeling.* Econometric Society Monographs no. 18. Cambridge: Cambridge University Press.

Sahlins, Marshall D. 1976. *Culture and practical reason.* Chicago: University of Chicago Press.

Sattinger, Michael. 1975. Comparative advantage and the distribution of earnings and abilities. *Econometrica* 43, no. 3: 455–468.

Schelling, Thomas C. 1978. *Micromotives and macrobehavior.* New York: Norton.

Smith v. Chanel, Inc. 1968. 402 F.2d 562 (9th Cir.).

Solon, Gary. 1992. Intergenerational income mobility in the United States. *American Economic Review* 82, no. 3 (June): 393–408.

Tirole, Jean. 1988. *The theory of industrial organization.* Cambridge: MIT Press, 1988.

Topa, Giorgio. 1996. Social interactions, local spillovers and unemployment. Ph.D. dissertation, Department of Economics, University of Chicago. December.

Tuchman, Barbara W. 1978. *A distant mirror: The calamitous fourteenth century.* New York: Knopf.

Veblen, Thorstein. 1934. *The theory of the leisure class: An economic study of institutions.* New York: Modern Library.

Wall Street Journal. 1994. As leather gets cheaper, it loses its cool, p. B1.

———— 1995. How a book makes the bestseller lists, and how the bestseller lists make a book. September 7, p. B1.

Weiss, Yoram, and Chaim Fershtman. 1998. Social status and economic performance: A survey. *European Economic Review* 42, nos. 3–5 (May): 810–820.

Weiss, Yoram, and Robert J. Willis. 1997. Match quality, new information, and marital dissolution. *Journal of Labor Economics* 15, no. 1, pt. 2 (January): S293–329.

Author Index

Subject Index